State
of Craft

Contents

Welcome to State of Craft...

What, do you imagine, a state of craft looks like? Soft, knitted grass, fabric houses, appliquéd clouds. Maybe. Or perhaps you envisage a community of crafters. Some kind of craft cooperative with a "make do and mend" mantra? Where crocheted granny squares count as currency...

Is it even a physical place, or rather a state of mind? If so, what would it feel like? "I'm in a total state of craft at the moment." In that case, I'm often in a right state of craft. Fluff flying, threads trailing; boxes of fabric pulled out from under the bed and turned out all over the place.

Looking around the living room where most of this book has been sliced and slotted together, it's well on its way to being a state of craft. There's the box of craft projects you'll find on these pages, destined shortly (sadly, for me) to be mailed back to their respective makers; my 1950s Formica table that operates in turn as computer table and sewing station, currently piled high with craft-book research. Until the other day, my big jumper pouffe was resplendent next to the telly, but I emptied it out to take a photo of the inside and now there are four carrier bags of miscellaneous stuffing leaning against the sofa. Then there's the not-quite-finished upholstery project...

When I interviewed printmaker Sam Wingate for this book, I found a chair in a similar unfinished state in his living space. I told him about my chair. Turns out we both did the same learn-to-upholster evening course (at the School of Stuff in Dalston, London, incidentally). This struck me as a very "state of craft" moment. It suggested a community of people, however subtly linked, with half-made chairs – or patchwork quilts, or knitted scarves, or tapestry cushions – under way in their homes. All these people with a craft project on the go, some lingering for a moment (or several months, in my case), but always there to pick up – something to just "do".

Many of the contributors to this book, however, no longer craft exclusively at home, having made the leap to working out of a studio and earning a living from making stuff with their hands. They are the master crafters at the very heart of modern craft, and their creative practices are, in turn, fuelled by an increasing number of people seeking to express themselves through an individual handmade aesthetic – whether that is made by themselves or bought from someone in the knowledge that it is handmade. And with the growth of the internet and online marketplaces such as Etsy, these homespun industries have been able to break out into the world like never before.

Sam Wingate's chair also reminded me that craft is as much about learning and sharing new skills as it is a constant ticking over of creative projects. So even though Sam is a successful printmaker, he is also a novice, languishing upholsterer, in need of someone else's knowledge. The basis of this book, then, is simply, a passing on of skills. Indeed, this aspect of craft is age-old, as parents have always passed on these skills to their children. The format may have changed – how-to-knit videos on YouTube, sewing workshops in pubs – but the sentiment remains the same.

When the publisher of this book, Ziggy Hanaor, and I put together *Making Stuff: an Alternative Craft Book* with Black Dog Publishing in 2006, it felt a bit like a call to arms, inspired in itself by things such as Rachael Matthews' rock 'n' roll knitting club and Tatty Devine knitting on stage with those gaffa-tape-loving, Berlin-based art popsters Chicks on Speed. Now, though, it feels as if craft no longer needs to shout its handmade manifesto. Craft has mellowed, having firmly established its place in contemporary culture. We no longer associate craft fairs with church halls and knitted loo-roll holders. As Rachael Mathews points out, knitting has firmly cast off (excuse the pun) its grandma association – it's now just knitting again. We have reached modern craft's second, or even third wave. The furrows have been ploughed and craft is now an accepted element of modern culture. Nice work, first-wavers!

So while craft's popularity has undoubtedly grown, it's not a club, or a clique. You don't have to sign up to some craftster code of conduct and don espadrilles to crochet or pedal to craft class on a fixed-wheel bike. The very fact that the professional makers gathered together on these pages are willing to share their skills and ideas is testament to the inclusiveness of the craft scene today.

I like to think of crafting like cooking: simply creating something that you want from what's around you. There are master chefs and, well, the rest of us. And while some people seem to assimilate cooking skills as they grow up, others need a little more encouragement, following recipes at first, then maybe adding in their own flourishes – to taste. Craft is the same. (But if you make something tasty, it won't be wolfed down in a matter of moments.)

And like making food, making stuff is, without a doubt, a cool thing to do – in the way that doing something off your own back, for yourself, will always be cool, whether you follow the three-billion-people-have-this-cook-book recipe or make it up as you go along. Bish, bash, bosh – pukka! And all that.

This is the current state of craft. Now go forth and make!

Victoria Woodcock

How To...

How To... **Knit**

Yep, knitting. What to say? The craft that's received the most unlikely of rock n' roll makeovers, knitting is at the vanguard of the new-craft (or is that neo-craft?) movement – and rightly so. Here's why: it's cheap to take up, can be done pretty much anywhere (I still balk at the Canadian tale of someone knitting and running on a treadmill though), and once mastered can yield prodigious fashion items.

Knitting, I have learnt, is not for everyone. And it has a pain barrier. Struggling with all the dinky twists and turns can be frustrating for beginners. Once that pain barrier is broken through, however, it's a gentle, relaxing, rewarding pastime. But give it a go yourself. And it really, really helps to have a seasoned knitter on hand to help. The internet is also full of useful advice if you get in a yarn-needle jam.

The knit kit

Sticks

Knitting needles are made in a variety of materials – metal, plastic, bamboo and wood are the most common ones. Beginners should definitely steer towards bamboo and wood and shy away from metal; although bamboo and wooden needles can be slightly more pricey, the texture means that your stitches are less likely to slip around, making the process of learning to knit, literally, easier to get to grips with.

Needles also come in different lengths and thicknesses. The longer the needles, the more stitches you can fit on – so if you are knitting something big, like a snood, say, make sure your needles are nice and long. But what you really need to pay attention to is the width. In the UK the width is measured in mm (and by a different point system in the US) and is referred to as the needle size. The size you use depends on the thickness of your yarn – thicker needles for thicker yarn.

The bigger the needles, the bigger the stitches, and the quicker your knitting will grow! However, don't be tempted to use very large needles for your very first attempt; it is much harder to get the technique right when knitting with chunky needles. Go for 4mm to 6mm needles, with yarn to suit (see string).

String

You can knit with any long string, the most common being balls of yarn. The label will tell you everything you need to know about the yarn: what the fibre is (wool, cotton, acrylic etc) and, importantly, what size needles to use. It's pretty simple really, the thicker the yarn the thicker the needles you will need. Ask the shop assistant to help you match yarn and needles.

When starting to knit, opt for wool or acrylic (or a mix of the two) as they are soft and have a slight stretch. Stay away from rigid fibres such as cotton, which take some getting used to. Also, start off with a smooth yarn, without slubs or bobbles, as this will make it easier to see the individual stitches.

Things

Scissors, dressmakers' pins and a measuring tape will come in handy, and a yarn needle, a big chunky sewing needle with a blunt tip (sometimes called a bodkin, or a tapestry needle) is indispensable. Stitch markers are required for a number of the knitting projects in this book; they are small, usually plastic, loops that wrap around the needle alerting you to a certain point in the pattern. A row counter slips onto the end of a needle: turn the dial to note the number of rows you've knitted. And you'll almost certainly find use for a medium-sized crochet hook – this will help you to fix mistakes…

But just to complicate matters, here are some needles of a different nature:

Circular needles

Basically a slightly odd-looking combo of two sawn-off knitting needles and a piece of plastic string; the circular knitting needle is a cunning way of knitting round and round without edges, or "knitting in the round". The needles are measured by width in the same way as straight needles to match the thickness of yarn, but the length of the string between the two is also crucial, as this needs to match the circumference of the item you are creating. For example, a circular needle to knit a hat will need to be much shorter than the circular needle you would use to knit the body of a jumper. Patterns will advise on both measurements, so you'll know exactly what you need.

You can also use circular needles to knit back and forth in the usual way. This has its advantages, especially when knitting in tight spots, such as on public transport, as the motion is more compact than with straight needles – and there are no needle ends to bash against the person sitting next to you.

Double-pointed needles

Another way to knit in the round is by using four needles instead of two, knitting round a triangle shape of shorter-than-usual, double-pointed needles. This technique is used for small circular items such as socks, legwarmers and finger puppets.

Start with a slipknot

Every single knitting project begins with this one simple knot.

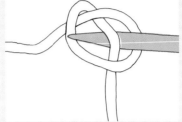

1. Pull out a length of yarn and make a loop, crossing over the yarn from the tail and the yarn that connects to the ball. Hold the point where they cross between your fingers.

2. Bring about 5cm-6cm of the yarn attached to the ball through the loop, catching up the yarn with either your fingers or a knitting needle, and forming a new loop. Keep hold of the new loop and let go of the original one.

3. Pull the tail end of the yarn tight to form a knot at the bottom of the loop. Place the loop on your knitting needle and pull both yarns so that the knot slips up to close the loop around the needle.

Double cast on (aka long-tail cast on)

The slipknot is the first loop and from here you just need to add a few more loops. There are various ways to do this, but the double cast on will work well for any knit, and it creates a stretchy edge too. As its pseudonym suggests, you need a long tail of yarn to do this – how long depends on the number of stitches you need to cast on. Multiply the number of stitches you need by three, then add another 20cm for good measure; pull out this length of yarn before you make the slipknot. This technique uses just one needle and is a bit tricky to learn – steps 3 and 4 in particular will require patience.

1. Hold the needle with the slipknot on in your right hand. With your left hand, hold the two yarns apart by bringing the tail end around your thumb and the yarn attached to the ball around your index finger. Run both yarns across the palm and hold them in place with your remaining left-hand fingers.

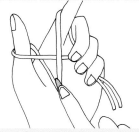

2. Bring the needle downwards and place the tip under the yarn that runs from thumb to palm, picking it up.

3. Making sure this yarn stays on the needle, bring the needle tip over the top of the yarn that runs from the index finger to the needle, then back round underneath this yarn, moving the needle towards the thumb.

4. Finally, move the needle through the space formed by the yarn running round the thumb.

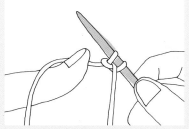

5. Move your thumb out of the loop and pull on the tail to tighten the new stitch you have created (don't pull too tight, the loop should be nicely snug).

Repeat steps 1-5 till you have the desired number of stitches.

This is knit

Knitting involves pulling one loop through another, over and over and over again. Before you try to knit an actual thing, just practise. The first few rows will be the most fiddly ones, and they can also be quite tight, which makes it more difficult to create the stitches. Try and keep the actions relaxed to make the loops a little looser.

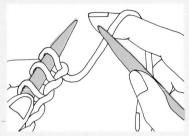

1. Hold the needle with the stitches on in your left hand, with the point beyond your thumb and index finger. Hold the empty needle in your right hand. The yarn (be careful that it is the one attached to the ball and not the tail) also goes in the right hand – you can weave it between your fingers to keep hold of it.

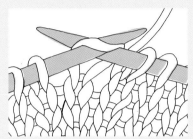

2. Stick the tip of the right-hand needle into the first loop, from left to right and from front to back.

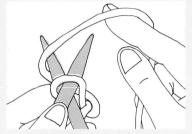

3. With the yarn at the back of the needles, wrap it around the point of the right-hand needle in a clockwise motion (underneath and then over the point). To keep the needles steady, grip both of them with your left hand, with the thumb at the front and the index and middle finger at the back.

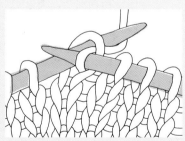

4. Take control of the right-hand needle again, and pull the yarn taut with your right hand too. Direct the point of the needle back out of the loop, from right to left and from back to front, bringing the yarn wrapped over the tip with it. You now have a new loop on the right-hand needle.

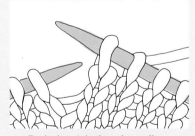

5. Push the right-hand needle a little further through the loop and move it to the right so that the original loop slides off the tip of the left-hand needle. This makes one whole stitch. Repeat steps 2-5 for each stitch on the row. At the end of the row, swap the needles from one hand to the other, and begin again on the other side of the fabric.

Purls of wisdom

A knit stitch looks like a "V" on the front of the fabric and a bump on the back, but sometimes you'll want to do a backwards knit stitch – a bump on the front and a "V" at the back. This back-to-front knit stitch is called a purl.

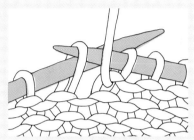

1. Hold the needle with all the stitches on in your left hand as for the knit stitch, but keep the yarn in front of the needles.

2. Insert the tip of the right-hand needle into the first loop, from back to front and from right to left.

3. Bring the yarn over the tip of the right-hand needle in an anti-clockwise motion, so that the yarn is still at the front of the needles.

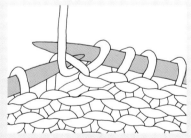

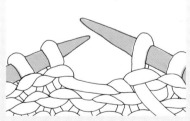

4. Direct the tip of the right-hand needle back out of the stitch, making sure that you bring the yarn wrapped over it back through the loop. You will now have a new loop on the right-hand needle.

5. As with the knit stitch, push the right-hand needle a little further through the new loop. Move the right-hand needle across to your right slightly to pull the original loop off the left-hand needle.

Repeat steps 2-5 for each stitch on the row.

Give them the slip

Sometimes you need to slip a stitch from the left-hand needle to the right without knitting it. This is usually used at the beginning of a row to make neat edges.

Follow steps 1-2 of knitting (page 12). Then, instead of wrapping the yarn round the needle, simply move the right-hand needle over to your right to bring the stitch off the left-hand needle. Consider that stitch slipped.

Mixing it up

Different patterns and effects can be created by combining knit and purl stitches. Here are the main examples:

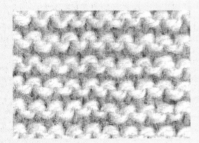

Garter stitch
The way to go for absolute beginners: knit every row. It has a nicely bumpy texture that would work for scarf.

Stockinette stitch
The majority of knitted clothes that you wear are made in stockinette stitch, which is created by knitting one row, then purling one row. This makes all the knit "V"s line up on the front, with all the purly bumps at the back. It's no good for scarves, however, as the edges tend to curl up.

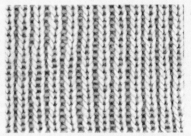

Rib
Knit one, purl one, knit one, and so one. This creates the stretched ribbed effect you get on cuffs. To switch from knit to purl on one row like this, you have to keep moving the yarn between the needle tips so that it's at the front for purling and at the back for knitting. There are variations on the basic rib too, such as knit two, purl two.

Ball change

When you get to the end of one ball of yarn, you need to keep on going with another. You use this same technique to introduce a new colour to make stripes The best place to do this is at the end of a row.

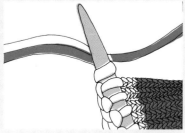

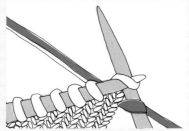

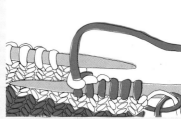

1. Cut the yarn, leaving a 15cm tail. Place the beginning of the new ball of yarn alongside the tail and hold them tightly together in your left hand.

2. Knit about six stitches using the new yarn, keeping hold of both yarn ends in your left hand.

3. Stop and knot the two tails together, firmly but not too tight. Carry on knitting. When the knit is complete, undo the joining knots and weave in the two ends separately for a bump-free finish.

Cast off

Once all knit up, you need to seal off the stitches – otherwise the whole thing will unwind. You can cast off in knit and purl, and it's much easier than casting on!

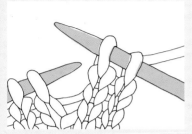

1. Knit (or purl) the first two stitches on the row as normal.

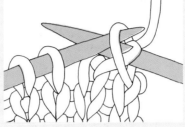

2. Then insert the left-hand needle into the front of the first stitch on the right-hand needle (the one you made first, and furthest away from the needle point). Lift the stitch over the second stitch (closest to the needle point).

3. Bring the stitch over the end of the needle and let go of it – it has been cast off.
4. Knit another stitch as normal and then repeat steps 2 and 3.

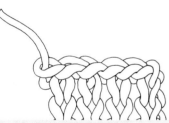

5. Continue in this way until you have only one stitch left on the right-hand needle. Cut the yarn with about 15cm spare, push the yarn end through the last loop, remove the needle and pull tight.

Working away

To secure the ends without leaving a big hulking knot, you do what is called weaving in or working away the ends. Untie the knots holding two yarn ends together and thread one loose end into a yarn needle (a large-eyed needle with a blunt end). Then weave the tail into the back of the knitted fabric for about 4cm-5cm. You can either push the needle through the loops along the edge, or work in and out of the stitches over two rows.

Gauging success

The gauge of a knitted fabric is the number of rows and stitches in a certain area. It is used to check that you are knitting to the same tension as the person who constructed the pattern and will ensure that your creation will be the correct size. This is less important when knitting something like a scarf, where the width and length won't alter the fit.

Some people knit tightly, others loosely. Before you begin a project, knit up a test square to check which size needles you need to knit to the tension demanded in the pattern. So, if you are a loose knitter, you might need smaller needles that suggested, whereas a wound-up-tight knitter may need larger needles.

1. Cast on 20-40 stitches (depending on the thickness of the yarn you're using – look at the label and cast on the amount it tells you the gauge will be plus another ten or so extra stitches) and knit until you have a square in the required stitch pattern.

2. Count the rows and stitches in a 10cm x 10cm area. Compare this to the gauge of the pattern, which will read something like "8 stitches and 12 rows over 10cm x 10cm". If your count is the same, then off you go! If you have fewer stitches, however, the stitches are too big and you need to do another swatch with smaller needles. Equally, if your count is too high, try again with needles one size larger. Keep going until you get it right. This may seem tedious, but is better than slaving over something that doesn't fit.

Knitting shorthand

Knitting patterns use a variety of abbreviations and you've got to get used to the lingo before you dive in. Here are the ones you'll come across in this book:

k	knit	st(s)	stitch(es)
p	purl	sl1	slip 1 stitch
m1	make 1 increase	rep	repeat
k2tog	knit 2 together	rnd	round
p2tog	purl 2 together	*	marks out an area to be repeated.

Fixer-uppers

When learning to knit, you'll no doubt make your fair share of mistakes. While slight imperfections can add charm, some – like gaping holes – are definitely to be avoided. And if you know how, most errors can be fixed.

Start on the right foot

Avoid the common mistake of creating an extra stitch at the beginning of the row by making sure you are knitting into the correct loop.

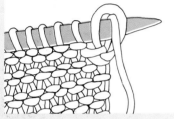 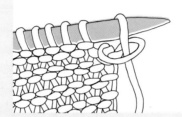

The knit stitch made on the last row can often be a bit loose and look like the first loops on the needle to knit into…

Push the stitch down to reveal the correct loop to knit into.

No more, no less

Count and keep counting how many stitches you have, this way you'll be able to detect a mistake pretty much as soon as it happens.

One too many stitches?

The easiest quick fix is to knit two stitches together to get you back on an even keel. Pro-knitters will tell you this is cheating – but who cares!

One too few stitches?

Chances are it has dropped off the needle somewhere… A dropped stitch is the most urgent of errors as it can lead to a big, gaping hole in your knit. Keep a crochet hook on hand to pick up the pieces.

Lost and found

If the stitch drops off the needle and you can still see the loop, quickly stick your needle back into the stitch, and move it back onto the left-hand needle to be knitted. Phew!

Lost in the wilderness

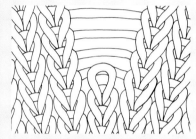 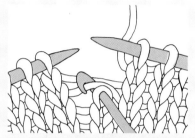 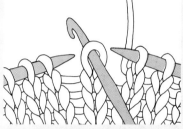

1. If your stitch has mysteriously disappeared, it will have unravelled down a number of rows. You have to find the lost loop, and pick it back up.

2. To do this properly you need to understand shapes of the stitches; you will see that some look like "V" shapes and others like bumps. Place the fabric in front of you so that the first stitch you want to make is a "V" (if it is a bump, turn the fabric over). Insert the crochet hook into the escaped loop from front to back and under the bar of yarn above it.

3. Hook the bar and pull it through the loop. Keep hold of this new loop you have formed.

4. Position the fabric so that you will be making a "V" again, and repeat steps 2 and 3 until there are no bars of yarn left.

5. Transfer the loop from the crochet hook back onto the left-hand needle. This is a tricky business for even experienced knitters, and you may find that you have mixed up the purls and knit stitches – at least there's no hole though.

Further off the straight and narrow

All the knit knowledge up to this point will have you reeling off perfect rectangles and squares, but for other shapes you need to be able to strategically increase and decrease the number of stitches on your needles: and this calls for a few more manoeuvres.

Decreasing

As with most things in knitting, there are a number of ways to decrease the number of stitches. The most common way to do this – also the easiest and the one you'll need for the patterns in this book – is to just knit two stitches at the same time.

Knit 2 together

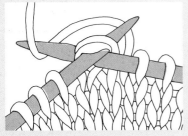

1. Ridiculously easy: just make a knit stitch in the usual way, but insert the needle through two loops instead of one. You'll be one stitch lighter. You can do this while purling also, which is called, surprisingly, purl 2 together, and is done in the same way by inserting the needle into two loops at once.

Increasing

To make a new stitch requires a little more effort. Here's one way to grow an extra loop.

Knit twice into one stitch

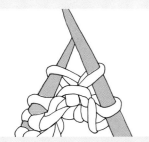  

1. Knit into the stitch in the usual way – insert the right-hand needle, wrap the yarn around and pull it through – but don't pull the original stitch off the left-hand needle.

2. Now push the right-handle needle through the back section of the loop on the left-hand needle, from front to back. Wrap the yarn around the needle tip as before and pull this out to form a second loop on the right-hand needle.

3. Pull the right-hand needle across to your right to pull the original loop off the left-hand needle. There are now two stitches on the right-hand needle, making a one-stitch increase.

Knitting in the round

There are two ways to knit round and round in a seamless tube.

Circular knitting needles

These do what they say on the packet and knit in circles. Just cast on the stitches as usual, so that they span across the plastic wire between the two needles. Make sure the stitches are all facing the same way and are not twisted, with all of the bumps of the cast-on edge pointing inwards, then join in the round. First, transfer the first stitch onto the last needle, so that it is next to the last stitch with the yarn tail; then pass this last stitch over the first one and onto the other needle.

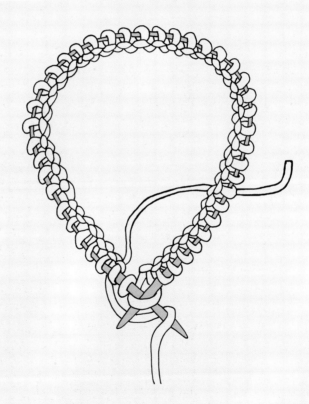

Knitting on four needles

Woah, hang on: four needles? Yep, knitting on four double-pointed needles (or dpns) is how you make tubes for socks, gloves etc. As with circular needles, you knit round and round continuously. Wielding four needles has got to be twice as complicated as knitting on two, I hear you say. Well, not really. It's a little tricky at first, so whatever you do, don't attempt this with slippy metal needles.

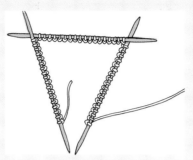 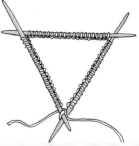

1. Cast on the desired number of stitches onto one needle in the usual manner.
2. Now divide the stitches onto three needles. Place a second needle into the first stitch, transferring it to the new needle. Keep repeating this step, transferring stitches one by one, until a third of the stitches are on the new needle.

3. Do the same from the other end, transferring a third of the stitches onto the third needle. You should now have an equal number of stitches on three needles.

4. Now you want to join the two ends to form a triangle. Make sure the stitches are all facing the same way and are not twisted, with all of the bumps of the cast-on edge pointing inwards, then swap the places of the first and last stitches. First, transfer the first stitch onto the last needle, so that it is next to the last stitch with the yarn tail; then pass this last stitch over the first one and onto the other needle.

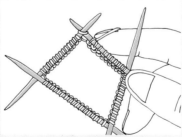

5. Now, take the fourth needle and use it to knit as usual, transferring the stitches to the new needle. Knit round and round, pulling the yarn tightly as you move from one needle to the other to keep gaps at bay. You can place a marker to indicate the beginning of the round, or just look out for the yarn tail. By the third round you'll be well away: knitting on four needles baby!

Joined-up knitting

Often knitting pieces need to be joined together, much like pieces of fabric. Don't, however, be tempted to hop on a sewing machine; knitting has its own versions of sewing, and they use a blunt needle.

Backstitch

The backstitch is strong and sturdy, and can be used on any edges. What's more, it's really quite easy. Use the yarn you knitted with and a big, blunt yarn needle.

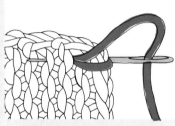

1. Place the right sides of the knit pieces together and pin, matching up the rows. Working at least one knit stitch in from the top edge, bring the yarn from back to front about 0.5cm from the side edge, through both layers, and attach by making a stitch round the side edge, bringing the needle up in the same spot. Then loop the needle round the side edge again and bring it up, from back to front, 0.5cm in front of the last stitch. Pull the thread through.

2. Now back track (hence the name), pushing the needle into the fabric at the end of the last stitch and bringing the needle up about 0.5cm further along than last time (where the yarn is).

Repeat step 2 until you have sewn along the whole seam. If you are using chunky yarn, make bigger stitches.

Mattress stitch

This is the method to use when joining together two side seams – and very elegant it is too.

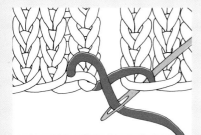

1. Place the two seams in front of you, side by side. Attach the yarn to the bottom corner of the right-hand piece (leaving a 15cm tail to weave in later), bringing the needle up from the wrong side to the right. Then make a figure of eight by bringing the needle up from wrong side to right on the corner of the left-hand fabric, then again on the right. Pull tight.

2. With the right sides of the fabrics facing upwards, use your fingers to pull the bumpy edge of the seam away from the knit piece. You'll see a ladder of horizontal bars.

3. All you do is push the needle under two bars on one side...

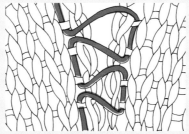

4. ...and then under two bars on the other.

5. Do this all along the seam, always switching from one side to the other. Pull tight, and the stitches will disappear. Finish with another figure eight to secure.

How To... **French Knit**

Is French knitting somehow just that bit more chic than bog-standard knitting? Well, no, not really. In fact, it's a little bit strange, as it produces only thin tubes of knitting, for which it can be quite difficult to find a purpose – until now, that is, as two projects in this book use French knitting to *très bien* effect. It's also lots of fun to do, and doesn't use knitting needles. Instead you use a knitting dolly...

Like this little fella! They can be found in yarn stores and toyshops.

Or you can make your own French knitting machine: stick four barrel-shaped drawing pins evenly around the top of a wooden cotton reel.

All you'll need otherwise is a big blunt needle or a crochet hook.

Le cast on

1. Thread the yarn through the reel, from top (where the pins are) to bottom.

2. Keeping hold of the yarn tail at the bottom with one hand, wrap the yarn at the top anticlockwise around one of the pins. Bring the yarn over to the left-hand side of the next pin clockwise.

3. Wrap the yarn anticlockwise around the next pin, and repeat until each pin has a loop around it.

Knitting *à la française*

By hooking loops off the pins and into the centre of the reel, a knitted tube will appear.

 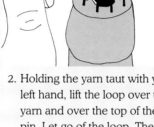 

1. Continuing to work clockwise around the reel, pull the yarn across the front of the first pin above the original loop. Use a needle (or a crochet hook) to pick up the original loop.

2. Holding the yarn taut with your left hand, lift the loop over the yarn and over the top of the pin. Let go of the loop. The yarn pulled across the pin will now have formed a new loop on the pin. There should be one loop on each pin at all times.

3. Repeat steps 1-2 on the next pin around clockwise. Work round and round the reel in this way. After every few stitches, pull the yarn tail at the bottom of the reel to encourage the knit tube to emerge.

Le cast off

1. When the tube is the desired length, lift up a loop without passing the yarn across the pin, and place it onto the next pin around clockwise.

2. Lift the bottom loop on the pin over the higher loop and the top of the pin.

3. Repeat steps 2 and 3 until there is just one loop left. Cut the yarn with a 10cm or so tail, lift the last loop off the pin and thread the tail through the loop to secure.

How To... **Make pom-poms**

Pretty much everyone must have made a pom-pom at some point or other. You remember stuffing wool through the middle of the doughnut-shaped bits of cardboard right? Well, with the help of two quick "pie slice" snips, the fluffy-ball process is made a whole lot easier.

Materials
~ yarns – knitting yarns are the most usual, but you can use strips of old T-shirts, plastic bags, silk scarves... anything long, thin and flexible
~ cardboard, such as an old cereal or shoe box

Tools
~ set of compasses
~ ruler
~ sharp scissors

1. The pom-pom maker is made up of two cardboard discs (like flat doughnuts). For each disc you need to draw two circles, one inside the other. The smaller inner circle should be about 2.5 times smaller than the outer one. With the compasses, draw out the circles twice. Here are some example sizes:

Pom-pom size	Radius of outer circle	Radius of inner circle
Small	2cm	0.8cm
Medium	3cm	1.2cm
Large	4cm	1.6cm
Extra-large	5cm	2cm

(The radius is the distance between the centre and the edge of the circle: this is the distance you set the compasses to.)

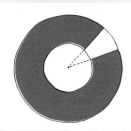  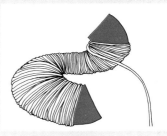

2. With a ruler, draw two lines from the centre to the edge of the circle, quite close together, like a thin slice of pie. Repeat on the other circle. Cut out around the outer circles; then cut out the pie slices and the inner circles.

3. Place the discs on top of one another so that the slits are aligned. Now start to wrap the yarn around the disc, using the slit to get into the centre. To speed things up, you can use a couple of yarn strands at once (if they are different colours you'll get a speckled pom-pom).

4. As the disc fills up, you can bend it to make it easier to wrap the yarn around.

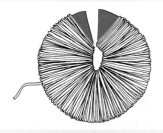  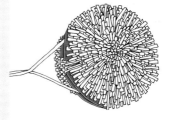

5. Wrap and wrap until the cardboard is covered with lots of yarn layers and the centre hole is nearly filled with yarn. Then cut the yarn and secure by pulling it under a few wraps.

6. To make the pom-pom you need to cut through all the wraps. Starting at the slit, wiggle the scissors in between the two layers of cardboard (it helps to place the pom-pom disc on a flat surface and a mug or jar on top), then cut through all the strands, working your way around the disc.

7. Cut a 30cm or so strand of yarn. Work the yarn in between the two cardboard discs, so that it wraps around the pom-pom. Pull the ends tightly so that all the cut strands gather into the centre of the disc. Tie as tightly as you can. Wrap the yarn around again, and tie a few more knots.

8. Remove the discs and fluff up the pom-pom. Trim any stray strands and uneven areas.

How To... **Sew**

From decorative embroidery to constructive dressmaking, hand to machine stitching, sewing encompasses a whole realm of creative opportunities. Bags, toys, capes, cushions or even animal ears; with the basic know-how of sewing a seam with a straight stitch, your making power is increased two-fold.

People tend to think sewing is super-complicated. Homemade clothes are greeted with amazement, which is nice if you're the maker, but the truth of the matter is that it's not rocket science. After all, once upon a time, people thought nothing of running up a frock or a shirt. And unlike knitting and crochet, you really can just dive straight in and learn as you go – with an unpicker in your pocket.

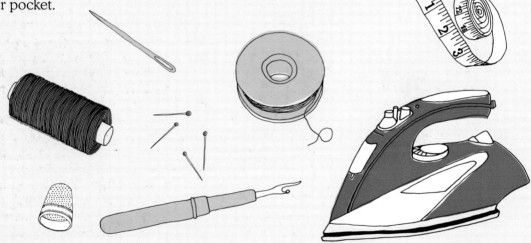

The stitch kit

Fabric
From cottons and silks to toweling and tweed, fabrics come in myriad colours, textures, patterns and thicknesses – all of which can be somewhat overwhelming to the uninitiated. When starting out, stick to a fairly sturdy cotton fabric, which is easy to handle and sew, and avoid stretchy or silky, shiny fabrics – they require a little more skill and know-how.

The rolls of fabric also come in different widths, which you'll need to factor in when buying enough fabric for your project. Take your measurements with you to the shop, and ask a sales assistant – they'll know their stuff.

Sewing fabric can also be sourced from old clothes. Why not turn an old skirt into a clutch bag? Again, shy away from garments with too much give or stretch.

Felt is great for adding embellishments, as the edges won't fray (you can make your own felt by throwing old jumpers in a hot wash). Interfacing is another useful fabric, which is used to back-up your outer fabric, stiffening and thickening it. It comes in an especially handy iron-on fusible format, and in varying thicknesses.

Thread

Sewing threads are most commonly made of cotton or polyester. They too come in different thicknesses, and all those millions of colours. Unless otherwise stated, opt for the "all purpose" sewing thread – you can't really go wrong.

Haberdashery

All the bits and bobs that embellish a sewing project are found in the haberdashery department, from practical buttons and zips to decorative lace, ribbon, pom-pom-edged trim, sequins… it's like being a kid in a sweet shop.

Needles

Sewing needles come in a range of lengths of thicknesses; get a set that has a selection for all occasions. Their names tend to explain what they are used for: leather needle, embroidery needle etc. For sewing woven fabrics, you need sharp points (as opposed to ballpoint needles, which are used on knitted, stretchy material such as jersey – good for embellishing a T-shirt with sequins, for example).

Scissors

Dressmakers have their own special scissors for cutting fabric – and woe betide those who use them to cut paper. They are worth investing in if you find yourself big into sewing (especially if you're going down the clothing route), but a pair of standard – fairly large and sharp – scissors will do the job.

Pinking shears

Not essential kit for the beginner, pinking shears are scissors whose blades are saw-toothed rather than straight, leaving a zigzag edge to fabric. This minimises the amount that a woven fabric will fray – and it can also be used for decorative purposes.

Dressmakers' pins

Essential for nearly all sewing projects, pins keep two layers of fabric in place as you work. Again they come in different lengths and thicknesses, for different fabrics and tasks, but the standard ones for medium-weight fabric – with either coloured heads, making them easier to see, or in plain metal – work well for general use.

Tailors' chalk

In a square or triangle shape with shaped edges, tailors' chalk is useful for drawing out patterns on fabric, as it can simply be brushed off. You can also use special fabric marker pens, which are designed so that the ink washes off or magically disappears, or just use a regular pencil, as normally the pattern lines can't be seen once sewn.

Stitch ripper

AKA a stitch unpicker, this dinky little tool is the easiest way to undo stitches made in error. Don't begin without one…

Thimble

It might seem a little grannyish, but if you're sewing through thick fabric, your hands will thank you for it.

Iron

For neat-looking sewing, seams need to be pressed as you go, so make sure you have an iron to hand.

Tape measure

Yep, you got it – you need this to measure things. Hang it round your neck, and off you go… A long ruler is also handy for drawing out large pattern pieces.

Sewing machine

Last but certainly not least, the sewing machine is the daddy of all sewing equipment. You certainly don't need one to get stitching (and lots of the projects in this book can be worked by hand), but when it comes to large projects and long seams, the sewing machine really comes into its own, quickly reeling out strong straight lines of stitches.

Before you get set to invest, have a go on a friend's machine first and get them to give you a tutorial. Each sewing machine differs slightly in the way it is threaded up and in the positioning of the dials etc; it's simply a case of getting to know your specific model, and diving into the manual from time to time. Looked after properly, sewing machines can keep on working for years. If things get a little wonky, stitch-wise send it to your local shop for an MOT and it should come back good as new.

Stuff to know before you sew

The right side of the fabric

Most fabrics will have a right side, and therefore also a wrong side. It's important to work this out for your chosen fabric straight off the bat, as this is always referred to in patterns. Take a good look at the fabric and decide which side you want to show to the world – this is the right side. (If you really can't tell, then no one else will be able to either, so just take your pick.)

One of the most common sewing commandments you'll come across is "with right sides facing" or "with right sides together". Both mean the same thing: place two pieces of fabric together so that the designated right sides are touching, and the wrong side of the fabric is facing out towards you. Seams are constructed on the wrong side of the fabric and then turned "right side out", so that the right side of the fabric is on the outside, with the rough edges where they belong, on the inside with the wrong side of the fabric.

The grain of the fabric

Take a good look at your (non-stretchy) fabric; you should be able to see thousands of lines of threads that are woven together to form the material. The threads run lengthwise and crosswise, or up and down and from side to side, at a right (90°) angle to each other – this is the grain of the fabric. When you position a pattern on fabric you want these lines to run straight through the pattern piece with any straight edges lining up along the grain. This is easy when you have a whole piece of fabric cut from a roll, as the lines that make up the grain will run parallel and at a right angle to the finished, uncut edges (also know as the selvage) – on a scrap you'll need to look more closely, however.

How to actually sew

By hand

Thread the needle

Cut a length of thread about 30cm-40cm long – any longer and it will start to get tangled up. Angle the thread through the eye of the needle and pull about 10cm through. Tie two or three knots at the other end, and you're away.

Normally, you want to sew with just one thickness of thread, but sometimes, when sewing on a button for example, it helps to double up the thread. In this case, cut a 60cm length of thread and pull half through the needle so that the two ends meet. Make a knot at the end with both lengths.

At the end of your sewn line, you must remember to secure the stitches before you cut the thread: tie a few knots or make a few stitches in the same spot.

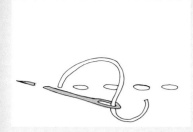

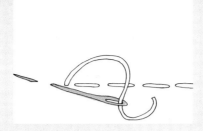

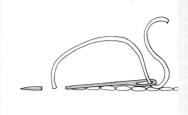

Running stitch

The general use-a-day stitch that resembles a line of dashes, the running stitch is used to form virtually all seams. Bring the needle up through the fabric, and pull it through up to the knot. Dip the needlepoint into the fabric and bring it back up a few millimetres further along; pull the thread through and you've made one stitch. Continue running the needle in and out of the fabric in a linear fashion. When you get faster, you can wiggle the needle in and out of the fabric several times before pulling the thread though, making several stitches at once.

Basting stitch

Exactly the same as the running stitch, except the individual stitches are longer to make a loose join, also known as tacking, which is used to hold two pieces of fabric together before sewing finally (sometimes on a machine).

Backstitch

This is the strongest hand-stitch. It forms a continuous line and is sometimes used for decorative purposes. Work backstitch from right to left. Bring the needle up from the back of the fabric, then make the first stitch by pushing the needle into the fabric behind (to the right of) the thread, and bringing it back up in front of (to the left of) the thread, by the same distance. Keep repeating the action, bringing the needle back to the previous stitch each time.

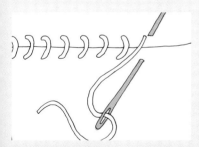

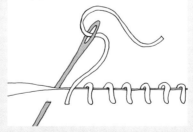

Overhand stitch

When sewing one piece of fabric on top of the other, as in appliqué or when sewing a hem, you use an overhand stitch. Push the needle into the single layer of fabric, then bring it up in the two layers. Repeat to make a track of stitches over the fabric join.

Whipstitch

An overhand stitch that is used to join two finished edges on the right side of the fabric is referred to as a whipstitch. Bring the needle from one side to the other, then bring the needle over the top of the join and pass the needle through the fabric in the same direction as before.

By machine

Threading up a machine is a little more complicated than threading a needle, and you need to thread up the top as well as the bobbin at the bottom. You'll need to look at the machine manual or get someone to show you how to do this, as all machines vary.

Instead of knotting to secure a line of stitches, as in hand sewing, with a machine you use a little manouevre called the back tack, which uses the sewing machines reverse setting – usually an easy-to-push-down switch. Sew forward for a few centimeters, then reverse back over the stitches before sewing forward again along the seam. Do the same at the end to secure.

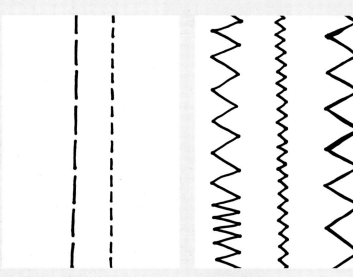

Straight stitch

This run-of-the-mill, everyday stitch is the machine version of a running stitch. If ever you are told to "sew", this is the stitch you need. You can alter the length of the stitch. Regular stitches in woven fabric should be set to 2.5mm.

Zigzag stitch

Making V-shaped stiches, a zigzag line can be used for decoration and in place of a hand-sewn overhand stitch for appliqué. It can also be used directly along a fabric edge to stop it from fraying. Here you can alter both the length of the stitches (the height of the V-shapes) and how far apart they are (wide or narrow V-shapes).

Construction

Seams

Seams are the bedrock of constructive sewing – the way to join one bit of fabric to another. They are worked on the wrong side of the fabric. The easiest way to understand how seams work is with a quick experiment: cut out two rectangles of fabric (along the grain, of course) and place them right sides together. Place a few pins through the two layers to hold them together and sew a straight line (either a running stitch or a straight stitch on a machine) roughly 1cm in from one edge. Remove the pins and open right side out. You've joined two pieces with a seam.

Seam allowance

This is the term used to describe the distance between the edge of the fabric and where you sew. So the example to the left created a seam with a 1cm seam allowance.

Notching into curved seams

If you sew a seam that has a curve, you'll need to "notch" the seam allowance to allow the fabric to move into the shape. All you do is cut small V-shapes out of the fabric, snipping close to the sewn seam but taking care not to cut into the stitches.

Hem

A hem is a neat edge of fabric where the rough edge is entirely hidden by being folded over twice.

Topstitch

When you sew a straight line on the right side it is sometimes referred to as a topstitch – essentially just a straight or running stitch that you can see on the outside of the finished item to add detail or force the fabric to lay in a certain direction.

Decorative stitches

These can be worked in regular sewing thread, embroidery thread or knitting yarns for a chunky look. Embroidery thread is usually made up of six strands, which can be separated out to create lines of different thicknesses.

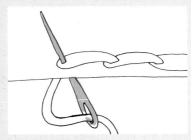

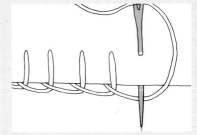

Appliqué

This is a technique of attaching fabric shapes to a base fabric. You can use any fabric for the shapes; felt works well as the edges don't fray, or you can cut out woven fabric with pinking shears (for a very neat look, you can turn under the edges). It also helps to stiffen the fabric shape with iron-on interfacing before cutting out. Simply pin the shape onto the base fabric and stitch all around the edge with an overhand stitch (or a blanket stitch – see right). Use matching or contrasting coloured thread, sewing or embroidery thread for different effects. You can also sew around the shape edge with a zigzag stitch on a sewing machine.

Split stitch

This stitch creates a continuous line and is a good place to start with embroidery as it can be used to recreate any line drawing in a stitched format. All you need to do is make one small stitch, keeping the needle at the back of the fabric; then bring the needle back up through the centre of this stitch, splitting it in two. Make another stitch, then bring the needle up again through this stitch, and so on.

Blanket stitch

You'll sometimes see this stitch worked in a contrasting colour around woolen blankets, but it can, of course, be used to create a decoration along any sturdy edge. Working from left to right, bring the needle up from the wrong to the right side of the fabric a little distance from the edge. At the same distance from the edge a little further to the right, put the needle into the fabric from right side to wrong side, then bring the needle around the edge and over the top of the thread. Pull tight then make another stitch to the right, the same distance from the edge, and continue in this way.

Buttons

You might not be at the button-hole-making stage yet, but buttons can be sewn on cushions, bags, T-shirts etc, where no fastening is required – purely for decoration. Here are the basics on buttons:

1. Thread a needle, doubling up the thread. At the spot where you want the button, make a stitch on the right side of the fabric, pulling the thread through to the knot.

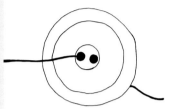

2. Push the needle through one of the holes in the button, from back to front, and push the button up to the fabric.

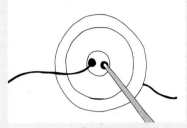

3. Push the needle through the other hole to the back of the fabric.

4. Bring the needle back to the right side of the fabric through the first hole; then back to the wrong side through the second hole. Repeat this action till the button is secure, make a few stitches on the wrong side behind the button before snipping off the excess thread.

How To... **Cross-stitch**

From personal messages to subversive statements, cross-stitch has got a lot to say for itself. And it's easy. Probably the biggest problem you'll encounter will be miscounting the squares on the chart... so count twice, then xxxxxxx!

The cross-stitch kit

Cross-stitch fabric
Known as Aida canvas, this is a specially woven fabric that has holes, arranged in squares, for you to stitch into. It comes in different "counts", which denote the number of stitches that can be completed per inch of fabric.

Embroidery floss
The thread for embroidery consists of six strands of thread twisted together and is usually sold in 8m hanks, or skeins. Depending on the count of the fabric you are using, the threads will be divided up; so you might use just two or three strands at once.

Tapestry needle
It's best, though not crucial, to use a needle with a blunt tip, such as a tapestry needle, so that you don't push the point through the fabric next to the hole.

Embroidery hoop
Holding the canvas taut, an embroidery hoop will help you to see the holes and ensure even stitching. They too come in different sizes – a 13cm or 15cm one would be good to start with – and in wood and plastic.

Scissors
You can get special curved-tip embroidery scissors to snip off the excess threads, but really any small scissors will do.

How to cross-stitch

If you're using a hoop, pop the fabric between the two layers, then pull it taut and even. Cut a length of embroidery thread about 40cm long, and divide the strands as required.

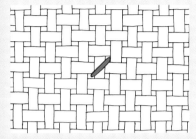

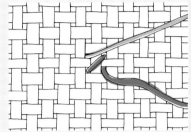

TIP

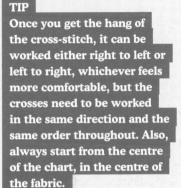

Once you get the hang of the cross-stitch, it can be worked either right to left or left to right, whichever feels more comfortable, but the crosses need to be worked in the same direction and the same order throughout. Also, always start from the centre of the chart, in the centre of the fabric.

Half stitch

The X-shape of cross-stitch is formed over one square in the fabric, one half of the X at a time. To form the first half, bring the needle from the back to the front of the fabric, then push the needle into the upper right-hand corner of the square, creating a diagonal stitch.

Full cross-stitch

Now bring the needle through the bottom right-hand hole and pull the embroidery floss through. Finally, push the needle to the back again through the top left-hand corner, forming an X.

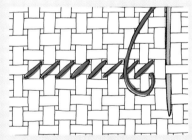

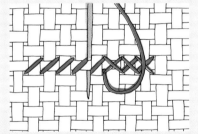

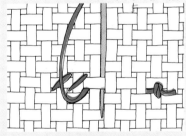

More than one X at a time

To speed things up, you can work a horizontal row of half stitches first. Make the first half stitch then bring the needle to the front as if to make a cross; instead, however, push the needle into the top right-hand corner of the next square along, and bring it back out of the hole vertically underneath. Repeat until you have the correct number of stitches.

Now work back across the row, right to left, completing the crosses. With the same vertical movement, push the needle to the back of the fabric through the top left-hand corner and back up through the bottom left-hand corner. Hop to the next row.

Securing threads – and no knots!

Tie a knot in the end of the thread – this is a waste knot and will be cut off later. Push the needle into the fabric from front to back about 3cm to the right of where you want to make your first stitch. Then move across to the left to make your first half stitch. Work across this row catching the thread at the back in the stitch, then cut off the knot. When you want to change colour or start a new thread, secure the end by running 3cm of thread under the stitches at the back.

How To... **Crochet**

Knitting's closest rival (or best friend, depending on how you look at it), crochet too has undergone a modern revival. Requiring just one hook in the place of two needles makes crochet the more compact and commuter-friendly of the two yarn-based crafts. It also creates a thicker fabric than knitting and, with just one live loop on the hook at any one time, comes with little risk of dropped stitches.

I learnt on Wikipedia that "crochet patterns have an underlying mathematical structure and have been used to illustrate shapes in hyperbolic geometry". So, yeah, cool. And you can make granny squares with crochet.

But just like knitting, crochet comes with a clutch of manoeuvres to master. Once you're up and running, however, the general consensus is that hook beats sticks in the speed stakes. Go!

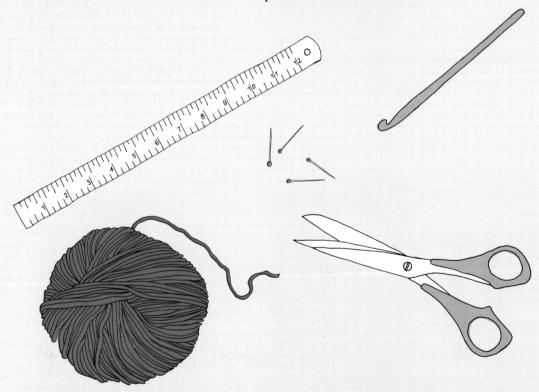

The crochet kit

Hooks
Crochet hooks, like knitting needles, come in materials such as metal, plastic and bamboo, the latter being easiest to get to grips with for beginners. They also come in different sizes, measured in millimetres (and by a different point system in the US). The size you use depends on the thickness of your yarn – larger hooks for thicker yarn.

String
Anything you can knit with you can also crochet with, the most common being balls of yarn. The label will tell you everything you need to know about the yarn: what the fibre is (wool, cotton, acrylic etc) and, importantly, what size hook to use. When starting out, opt for wool or acrylic (or a mix of the two) as they are soft and have a slight stretch.

Things
Scissors, dressmakers' pins and a measuring tape or ruler will come in handy, and a yarn needle (a big chunky sewing needle with a blunt tip) is indispensable.

Getting to grips with hook and string

The crucial thing about crochet is to hold the hook comfortably and the yarn with enough tension so that when you when you catch the yarn it stays firmly in the lip of the hook. Hold the hook in one hand, gripping it either like a pencil or a knife; and hold the yarn in the other, wiggling it in between your fingers to hold it tight. Use whichever method feels more comfortable.

Start with a slipknot

Every crochet project begins with this one simple knot.

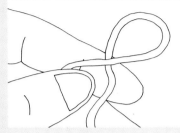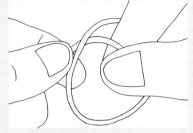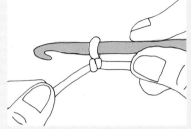

1. Pull out a length of yarn and make a loop, crossing over the yarn from the tail and the yarn that connects to the ball. Hold the point where they cross between your fingers.

2. With your spare hand, stick your thumb and index finger through the loop, pinch hold of the yarn attached to the ball and bring it back out, forming a second loop. Keep hold of the new loop and let go of the original one.

3. Pull the tail end tight to form a knot at the bottom of the loop. Place the loop on the hook and pull both yarns so that the knot slips up to close the loop around the needle.

Foundation chain

The basis of a crocheted fabric is a chain of stitches. The chain stitch is also used to produce spaces and loops in your fabric.

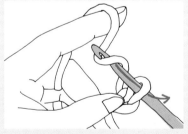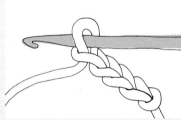

1. Hold the hook with the slipknot on it in your right hand. Hold the yarn taut with your left hand, looping the yarn from the ball over your index finger and gripping the tail end of the yarn at the bottom of the slipknot between thumb and middle finger. Bring the tip of the hook in front of the yarn, and under and around the yarn

2. Catching the yarn in the hook, draw the yarn through the loop on the hook: this makes one chain

3. To make the next chain, pull the yarn through the loop on the hook in the same way. Repeat until you have the number of chains required. Do not count the slipknot or the loop currently on your hook as chain stitches.

Slip Stitch

Worked across whole rows, slip stitch makes a very dense fabric and is therefore usually used to join the end and beginning of a round, or work along to a required position.

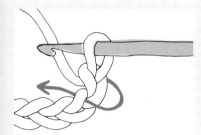 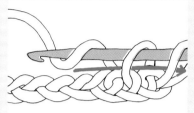 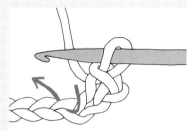

1. Make an extra chain (this is a turning chain) at the end of your foundation chain. Insert the hook into the centre of the second chain along, from front to back.

2. Wrap the yarn around the hook, from back to front, and draw the yarn through both the chain and the loop on the hook. This completes one slip stitch, leaving one loop on the hook.

3. Insert the hook in the centre of next chain, and repeat step 2.

4. Continue across the foundation chain in this way. To begin a second row, turn your work, then make one chain (turning chain) and work a slip stitch into the top of each stitch on the previous row.

Double Crochet

This stitch creates your common and general crochet fabric – flexible but still hardwearing. (Note: what is referred to as double crochet in the UK, is referred to in the US as single crochet – confusing!)

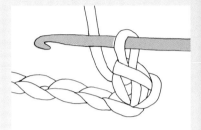

1. Make one extra chain on the foundation chain (this is the turning chain). Insert the hook into the second chain from the hook, wrap the yarn around the hook and draw it through the chain. You now have two loops on the hook.

2. Wrap the yarn around the hook again and pull the yarn through both loops on the hook. This makes one double crochet stitch.

3. To make the next stitch, insert the hook into the next chain along, and do the same again: draw a loop through, then hook the yarn through the two loops.

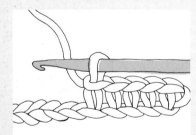

4. Work a double crochet into each of the remaining chains to complete the first row.

5. To make a second row of double crochet, turn the work so that the hook is at the right-hand side. And make one chain (turning chain). To make the first stitch, insert the hook through the top two loops of the first stitch. Continue working into every stitch in this way along the row, and on all following rows.

Treble crochet

Taller still than a double crochet stitch, treble crochet results in more open, more flexible fabric. It's worked in a similar way to double crochet, but you wrap the yarn around the hook before you begin the stitch. (On the confusing US/UK lingo front, treble crochet is referred to as double crochet in the US).

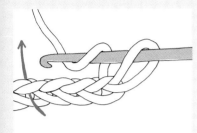

1. Make two extra chains on the foundation chain (this will count as the turning chain and you'll skip the first three chain stitches). Wrap the yarn over the hook once, then insert hook, from front to back, into the fourth chain along from the hook. There are now three loops on the hook.

2. Wrap the yarn around the hook again and pull the yarn through the first two loops. There are now two loops on the hook.

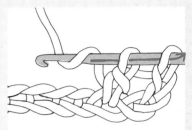

3. Now wrap the yarn over the hook once more and pull it through the two remaining loops on the hook. This completes one treble crochet stitch.

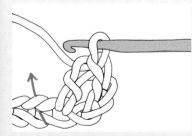

4. Wrap the yarn over the hook and insert it into the centre of the next chain, then repeat steps 2 and 3. Work a treble into each chain in this way.

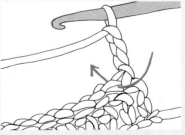

5. At the end of the row, make a chain of three for the turning chain, then skip the first stitch and work into the top of the second stitch along, inserting the hook under the top two loops. Make the treble stitches as before, from here on always catching the two loops on the stitch below.

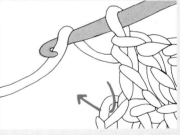

6. At the end of the row, work the last stitch into the top of the three-chain at the edge.

A bit about turning chains

As you will have seen, crochet stitches come in varying heights, and to start each row at the same height as the stitch you will be working, you must start with a chain, called the turning chain. It can be worked before or after turning your work. Usually, the turning chain takes the place of the first stitch, so after working the turning chain, you work into the second stitch along the row. Then when you come to the end of the row, you treat the turning chain as a stitch and work in it. For double crochet, however, the turning chain does not count as a stitch. After working the turning chain, you work into the first stitch below and do not work into the chain at the end.

Half treble and double treble

Variations on the double-treble theme, these are two more basic crochet stitches, though they aren't used in this book.

Working in rounds

As with knitting, you can work crochet in rounds rather than rows. The stitches are the same as when working in straight rows, but you join the two end of the foundation chain to form a circle – to make a hole in the centre that is drawn closed you usually use a chain of four to six stitches.

1. Make a chain, then insert the hook into the first chain you made.

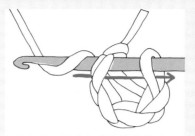

2. Wrap the yarn around the hook in the usual way, then pull the yarn through the chain and the loop, forming a ring of chain.

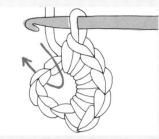

3. If you are working in double crochet, make one chain (if you're working in treble crochet, chain three). The first round is worked by inserting the hook into the centre of the ring (and not into the individual chains). Try to catch up the tail end of the yarn in the stitches so that you'll be able to close the hole tightly later.

4. You don't turn your work at the end of a round; just keep going round and round. To keep track of where the round begins, you can place a contrasting piece of yarn across the crochet and sandwich it in the first stitch. Work the second row as you would for a straight line, making a suitable turning chain and pushing the hook under the top two loops of each stitch.

Ball change

When you run out of yarn or want to change colour, you don't need to fasten off the old yarn, just pull through the new yarn when needed. Try to do this at the end of a row, into the last stitch, as this will create a neater appearance. When working in double crochet, simply insert the hook into the stitch as usual, but drop the old yarn and instead wrap the new yarn around the hook. Off you go! With other stitches, work through the stitch until there are two loops left on your hook, and then when you about to pull the yarn through for the last time to complete the stitch, switch to the new yarn. In both instances, simply continue with the new ball of yarn. You can tie a temporary knot and weave in the ends later with a yarn needle (as with knitting) or try to work over the ends, securing the yarn tails by catching them in the stitches.

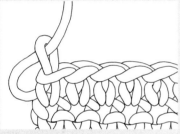

The end is in sight...
To stop all your hard work from literally coming undone, you just need to fasten off the last "live" loop. It's really easy: just cut the yarn to about 15cm and pull this yarn tail through the last loop. Pull tight, and it's all safe and secure. To tidy away the yarn ends, simply weave them into the fabric. Just thread up the yarn needle and run it under several nearby stitches for 4cm-5cm, then snip off the excess.

More or less

To shape your piece of crochet, you'll be required to increase or decrease the number of stitches on the row or round you're working on.

Increase

To increase the number of stitches in double or treble crochet you simply work two (or more) stitches into the same stitch on the row below. Complete one stitch fully, and then insert the hook back into the same opening and go again.

Decrease

To make a row shorter, there are various things you can do. Sometimes a pattern will call for you to work two stitches together. For the projects in this book, however, decreases are made by simply skipping over a stitch on the row below.

Feel the tension

Your tension is how tightly or loosely you crochet – and consequently, the size of the stitches you make. This varies from person to person, and sometimes you will need to alter the size of the hook you use to create the correct size stitches as demanded by a pattern. While you don't really need to delve into this for the projects in this book, if you get onto making garments it is really important to work this out in order to make the item to the correct size. As with knitting, this is worked out over a 10cm x 10cm square; you make a tester and count the number of stitches and rows in this area. If you count too many stitches, change to a larger hook size; too few and you need to use a smaller hook.

The short answer

When following crochet patterns, you've got to understand the shorthand... it's easy when you know the lingo.

ch	chain	*inc*	increase
dc	double crochet	*rem*	remaining
tr	treble crochet	*st(s)*	stitch(es)
sl st	slip stitch	*yrh*	yarn round hook
beg	beginning	*rep*	repeat
dec	decrease	*sk*	skip

Projects

Alice Gabb's **Captain Bert**

This hearty old chap must be saluted upon introduction.

Tools
~ dressmakers' pins
~ sewing needle
~ marker pen
~ scissors
~ stuffing tool: a long implement such as a knitting needle, chopstick or pencil
~ iron
~ sewing machine (optional)

Materials
~ A3 piece of cardboard
~ 25cm x 50cm of brown tweed or wool fabric
~ 25cm x 50 cm of cream wool blanket
~ 15cm x 30cm white cotton fabric
~ sewing thread in cream, light pink and black
~ polyester toy filling
~ medal or vintage accessory

What to do

1. Photocopy and enlarge the templates on page 228 so that the body is about 40cm high. Cut the shapes out of cardboard.
2. Mark out the arm template twice on the back of the cream blanket using a marker pen. Leave at least 3cm of fabric in between the two shapes. Place the marked out cream fabric over the tweed, making sure that both the "good sides" that you will want to show are facing the inside, and pin in place. Leaving 1cm of fabric around the lines, cut out the shapes.
3. Using a straight stitch on a sewing machine (or a running stitch if you are working by hand), sew along the lines, leaving the ends open (fig A).
4. Carefully turn the arms inside out; use your stuffing tool to help.
5. Stuff the arms tightly with the toy stuffing, again using the stuffing tool.

6. Repeating the same technique as step 2, mark out the body template on the cream blanket, but when cutting out the two layers, leave 3cm of fabric around the template.
7. Place the arms in between the cream and brown fabric half way down the body (fig B). Point the arms inwards so that the open ends are at the edge of the body, and make sure the tweed side of the arm is facing the tweed fabric. Pin the arms securely in place.
8. Carefully stitch around the body 3cm from the edge, leaving a space in between the legs for (ahem) stuffing. Be very careful when you get to the arms; it is tricky but go slowly, making sure you have captured the whole width of the arm.
9. Trim around the stitching, leaving 0.5cm-1cm around the edge. Snip little lines around the ears, being careful not to break the stitches (fig C).
10. Turn inside out and stuff – it takes a lot more stuffing than you might think. Keep using the stuffing tool, making sure you reach the ears and toes.
11. Once he is totally stuffed, the gap can be stitched up by hand with a whipstitch.
12. Using the face template and a biro, mark out two face shapes on the white cotton. Cut one out exactly on the line, and cut out the other 3cm from the pattern edge.

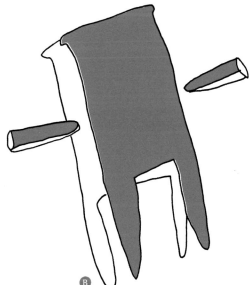

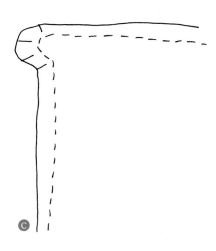

"Captain Bert likes a fine cigar or two but makes a loyal, trustworthy companion who will charm you with tales of his adventures."

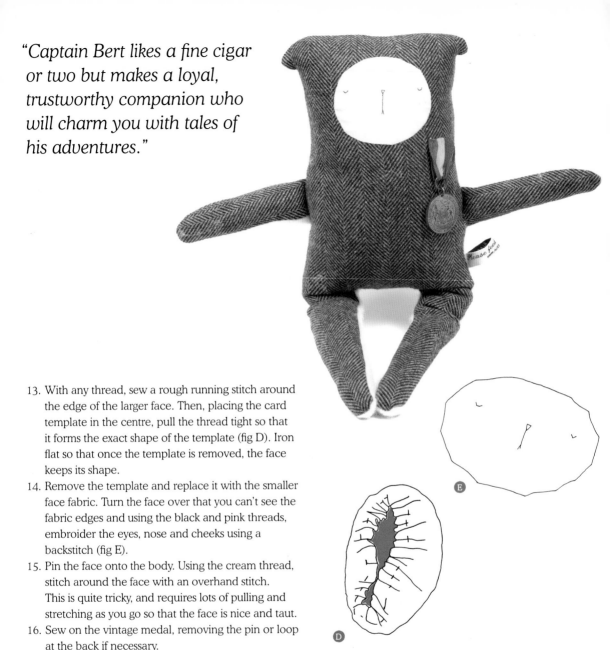

13. With any thread, sew a rough running stitch around the edge of the larger face. Then, placing the card template in the centre, pull the thread tight so that it forms the exact shape of the template (fig D). Iron flat so that once the template is removed, the face keeps its shape.
14. Remove the template and replace it with the smaller face fabric. Turn the face over that you can't see the fabric edges and using the black and pink threads, embroider the eyes, nose and cheeks using a backstitch (fig E).
15. Pin the face onto the body. Using the cream thread, stitch around the face with an overhand stitch. This is quite tricky, and requires lots of pulling and stretching as you go so that the face is nice and taut.
16. Sew on the vintage medal, removing the pin or loop at the back if necessary.

Alice Gabb is an illustrator living and working in Hackney, London. As well as making fine stationery, she particularly likes pictures of cats and the royal family. She spends her days screenprinting and hunting out vintage curiosities. *www.alicegabb.com*.

Kristen Cooper's
Knit & Knotted Hairgrips

Get to grips with French knitting, and some fancy finger work.

Tools
~ crochet hook
~ scissors
~ French knitting bobbin

Materials
~ any not-too-chunky knitting yarn in two different colours – aran-weight or 4-ply would work well
~ bobby-pin hairgrip

Skills
~ French knitting

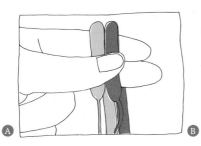
A

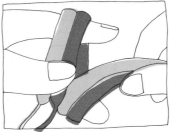
B

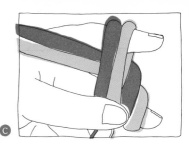
C

What to do

1. Take your bobbin and start French knitting, following the instructions on page 26. You need two strands of French-knitted cord approx 35cm long. This will take several hours, and is a good project for a train journey or while watching telly once you've got going.

2. Hold the top of the two cords of French knitting between your thumb and your index and middle fingers of your left hand (fig A).

3. Separate the index and middle fingers. Take the ends of the cords in your right hand and bring then round to the front of your index/middles fingers creating a complete loop with the start of the strand (fig B).

4. Bring the ends of the cords round the back of the loop, in between the middle and the index finger, and bring them up through the space created between two fingers to the left of the loop (fig C). Make sure not to twist the strands at any point.

5. At the front of the fingers, bring the yarn ends across to the right (fig D).

6. Repeat the action in step 4, bringing the yarn ends through the space created between the middle and index finger, from the back to the front of the hand (fig E).

7. Now bring the yarn ends through the bottom of the loop created around the index finger, from left to right (fig F).

8. Then bring the ends through the top of the loop created around the middle finger, from right to left (fig G).

9. Now the basic system of the knot is finished and just needs to be adjusted. Take the knot off your fingers (fig H).

10. Tighten the knot by following the strands from one end to the other, gently tightening each section as you go (fig I).

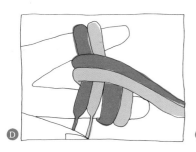
D

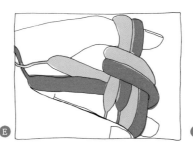
E

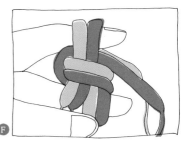
F

G

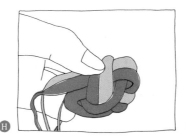
H

I

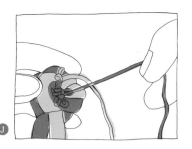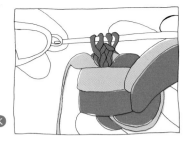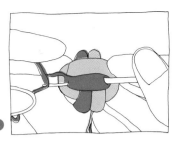

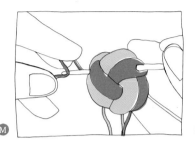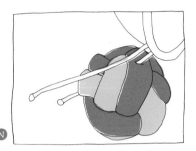

11. Cut the remaining four cord ends to approx 2cm in length. Keep adjusting until the knot is a nice shape.
12. Unwind the cut end of one cord until you reach a point that is overlapped by one of the outer cords of the knot (fig J).

13. At this point you want to tie off the yarn. Bring the crochet hook through all four loops that make up the strand; then hook the yarn end and pull it through the loops. Pull tight to secure.
14. Repeat steps 12 and 13 for the remaining three cords.
15. Hide the yarn ends inside the like-colored cord, by pushing the crochet hook into the cord and pulling the yarn into it (fig L).
16. Pull the yarn end out. Then push the crochet hook into the knot from the other side, again on a like-coloured section, so that the hook surfaces next to the yarn end. Pull the yarn through the middle of the knot (fig M). This process basically sews the knot together, and the more you weave the yarn ends through the knot, the more secure it will be.
17. Trim any leftover yarn ends. Now simply slide the knot onto a bobby-pin (fig N).

Kristen Cooper is from Los Angeles but now lives in Berlin with her husband. She works as an artist in several capacities: making installation and intervention artworks; hand-weaving and hand-dyeing textiles; and craftwork. *dawanda.com/shop/RedThread, www.kristencooperhandwovens.com, www.kristen-cooper.com.*

A Alicia's **Vintage Fabric Necklace**

By Anna Alicia Johnson

A simply stylish accessory to stitch up.

Tools

~ dressmakers' pins
~ sewing needle
~ ruler, or tape measure
~ scissors
~ sewing machine

Materials

~ approx 5cm x 75cm piece of lightweight vintage fabric; cotton works well, but most fabrics will be fine, as long as they are not stretchy
~ five chunky beads, approx 1.5cm-2cm wide
~ 3m of wool yarn
~ sewing threads to complement your fabric and wool

What to do

1. Cut a strip of fabric 5cm x 75cm.
2. Lay the fabric strip out, right side down, and starting at one end, fold in either side lengthways to meet in the middle.
3. Then fold the strip in half along the middle lengthways so the (already folded) edges meet. Pin in place all along the length of the strip (fig A).
4. Thread your sewing machine and set to a small zigzag stitch. Starting about 5mm from the end (this helps the machine feed the fabric through), sew along the open side of your folded-over strip close to the edge, removing the pins as you go. Then sew along the other edge to finish. This creates a strong ribbon of fabric, and a pretty zigzag pattern.
5. To add the beads, you'll need a length of wool approx 20cm long (or longer if you are using bigger beads), and a needle and thread. Place the end of the wool in the middle of one tip of the fabric ribbon and hand-stitch firmly in place (fig B). This will be covered, so it doesn't need to be neat.
6. Pinch together the edges of the fabric ribbon over the wool you have sewn in place (fig C), and hand-stitch together for about 1.5cm.
7. Thread the beads onto the wool (using a needle if they have small holes). Place the loose wool end in the middle of the other tip of the fabric ribbon so that the beads are held tight, but with enough slack to hang nicely. Hand-stitch the wool in place and cut off any excess. As before, pinch the edges together over the wool and stitch for 1.5cm.
8. Roughly 14cm in from each end, pinch the edges of the fabric together as you did at the tips, and hand-stitch along for about 1.5cm.

TIP
This necklace is made out of vintage kimono fabric, handmade ceramic beads and organic fairtrade wool, but you can use almost any scraps of fabric, old beads and odd bits of wool.

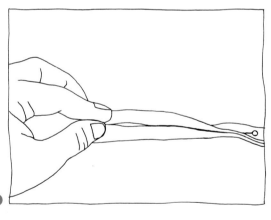

A

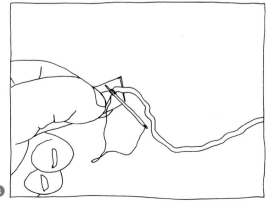

B

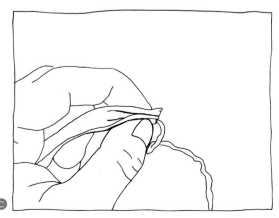

C

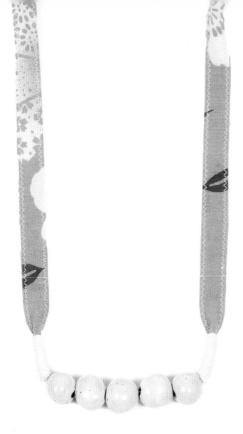

11. Do the same at the tips, but make sure you finish with the wool at the very end of the fabric ribbon. You need to neaten the ends so that no fabric is showing – this can be a little tricky. Continue wrapping the wool round, heading towards the string of beads in smaller circles, stitching the wool in place as you go (fig E). When the fabric is covered and the wool is secure, cut off any excess. Add a few extra stitches.

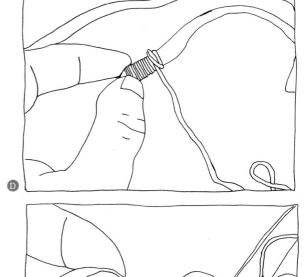

D

9. The "pinched" areas are now bound with wool. Cut four yarn lengths each about 75cm long. Start with one of the pinched areas 14cm from the beads; take a length of wool and hand-stitch the end to the top of the fabric, then wrap the wool around (covering the wool end), working your way to the bottom of the pinched area, then up and back down again (fig D). Once you are happy with the binding, hand-stitch down the end of the wool. Cut off any excess and add a few extra stitches over the loose end.

10. Repeat on the other side.

E

Anna Alicia Johnson lives and works in east London with her artist husband and lots of overgrown house plants. Her jewellery, homeware and wedding collections focus on vintage or ethically produced fabrics. Anna took a roundabout route to becoming a craftsperson, via a degree in art history and an MA in fine art. Her art background plays a huge role in inspiring her collections, as do the travels of her childhood and the buzz of London. *www.aalicia.bigcartel.com, www.aaliciawedding.bigcartel.com.*

Hannah Ayre's **Corking Hooks**

You've drunk the Champagne, recycled the bottle; but what about the cork? How about a handy hook?

Tools

~ pliers
~ hammer and nail, for fixing hooks to wood, or a drill and rawl plugs, for putting hooks into plaster

Materials

~ champagne corks (a group works well together, so get drinking)
~ double-ended screws with a point at both ends, such as 2in dowel screws (not always available in your local DIY shop, so you might need to try somewhere more specialised)

What to do

1. Decide where you wish to put your hook and mark the spot.
2. If screwing into wood, tap a nail a short way into the wood first, then remove it. If screwing into a wall, you will need to drill a hole and pop in a rawl plug, then screw the screw into that.
3. Since the screws have no head, you can't use a screwdriver: use pliers instead to drive the screw in half way.
4. Find the centre of the flat part of your cork, and simply twist the cork onto the protruding screw. And you're ready to hang things.

Hannah Ayre is a freelance artist working with a wide range of materials, usually reclaimed, and also runs community arts workshops for children and adults. She made these hooks to hang up tools in her shed, as after several years on a waiting list, she was recently given her own allotment plot – a brand new playground to indulge her creative eco-projects! *www.juliannagrove.com*.

Interview with Tatty Devine's Rosie Wolfenden and Harriet Vine

Rosie Wolfenden left and Harriet Vine, right.

Do you still crochet?

H: Yeah, I went on [BBC radio show] *Women's Hour* doing crochet. When Rachael [Matthews, of Prick Your Finger] was doing all the Late Views at the V&A [Museum], I used to go and help people learn how to knit and crochet. When *Women's Hour* phoned, we were making crocheted prawns and crocheted peas.

How did Tatty Devine come together?

H: Rosie and I met at art college. I was making paintings, quite normal ones, if you could call them that, and Rosie wasn't making paintings, she was sticking bits of glass and lenses together, making work with light and shadow. Tatty Devine happened completely by accident. One day I was wearing a bit of old belt that I'd made into a wristband. It was held together with a hairclip, it wasn't quality crafting by any stretch of the imagination. It was very haphazard. And everyone just went, "It's so cool, where's that from?"

Then coming home from the pub one night, I found about 18 sacks of leather outside an upholstery shop. There was every kind of leather, and bits of fabric, lighting fittings and stuff. It was like a crafting dream. We stacked it up in my bedroom and I got on with my course. At the end, we cut it up into little strips; we couldn't work out a way of fastening it together, so with my dad we cut this little arrowhead - pointy, two slashes - and then in the other end we put little slits, and the arrow through them. It was about as basic as you could get. We went to Camden Market; sold 10 and made 50 quid.

When did you start crafting?

R: I guess I've crafted all my life. When I was little I used to hang out with my granny, who wrote books on making stuff: how to sew, how to embroider, how to garden. She opened up a hotel on the Isle of Wight in the 1950s, which my parents took over, and she did all the furnishing herself - curtains, cushions, lampshades - she made everything. I had a special plot of garden that was mine. But after gardening, my granny and I would sit and do embroidery. She would sew me a dress and allow me to embroider the front of it.

H: It's one of my first memories, making stuff; it's what I used to do with my friends. I remember getting hundreds of circles of fabric, running stitches round them and making little bags, then threading them together to make clowns. All I did was make stuff. In Brownies once we had to make a teddy bear, by sewing two bits of felt together. It was probably meant to take the whole Brownie lesson but I did it in about 10 minutes, and Brown Owl [the Brownie leader] made me take it all apart and stitch it back up again, so I stitched it like an elf had stitched it. I did craft, and loads of crochet; miles of crochet.

Not bad! Then we used to make things with plectrums and just drill holes in things, spray stuff with spray paint, turn ping-pong balls into hair bobbles.

What's the best thing you've ever made?

R: When I was little I got really into patchwork. My granny used to wear patchwork dresses, and make patchwork tents - they were amazing. I think the best thing I've ever made is a patchwork quilt. Or I knitted a jumper once, which was quite insane. I also used to make clothes with my mum. We'd call it stressmaking, because I used to get so stressed. But I remember that I made this top and skirt in Laura Ashley material. It was quite nice. I was probably about 12. That was pretty good at the time. Probably awful actually, but relatively advanced.

And what's your best Tatty creation?

R: When we first made the plectrum jewellery, we were like, "That's such a great idea" - and it had never been done before. A lot of the things we do are a twist on something that's normal.

Are you ever amazed by the things you make?

H: Sometimes you are a bit shocked that you could have made something. I've been making stuff for 10 years, hundreds and hundreds of things a year, so you learn tricks, I suppose, that make things look like they're not handmade - that take it to a different level. Sometimes when I'm developing a collection, I make stuff and it looks like I've made it; then I change something and all of a sudden it takes on a life of its own. It's still handmade, but it's professionally handmade. There is a distinct difference, in a funny kind of way. Everything starts with me twiddling around with bits of card and string though.

You must see people out wearing your jewellery all the time now?

R: Yes, it's completely insane! I love seeing the way people wear it, because it's always different. Sometimes I go to a pub and then a restaurant and then the theatre, and I see someone in each space wearing Tatty - that's mental. I just never, ever thought that would happen. Everything we do has always been about trying to be individual, about making something that nobody else has got. And now I'll go out in Dalston and see five moustache necklaces. That's why we keep doing a collection, because it's really important to keep making stuff that doesn't exist yet. It's hard to retain a niche feel to things, and sometimes it's tempting to just run with it.

What is your biggest craft disaster?

H: There are loads of things every season that don't quite make it. There is one thing in particular I'm thinking of. For one collection we were all feeling a bit tropical and had the idea of an elephant's head with an articulated trunk. And on paper it sounds like a great idea, but in reality, it just was awful! I've got it somewhere. I cut it in wood. But the curves of an elephant's trunk, and the weight; it just didn't equate. It got left behind with this hilarious pile of things that never make it.

R: With Tatty, things are either immediate or they take ages. With the plectrums, for example, it was immediate, but sometimes it can take months of tweaking. We made some really big, gemmed owls recently, and they took three months to get right. They kept being not right; the wrong colour, the wrong size.

Where is your favourite place to come up with ideas?

H: It happens at all different times. It could be on the bus, or sometimes I just wake up in the middle of the night, literally with a jolt; or walking round the park, or in a car driving along. So much is going on all the time, that sometimes you can't hear your inner monologue. But in those quiet moments you get little waves. And then Rosie and I come together and we talk about random stuff that we both seem to be into, and I annotate it. We collect images and just pick up things, and it will gradually work its way into a design.

R: I'm more of an ideas person than a hands-on person really. And over the years at Tatty Devine, Harri's concentrated more on the making and I've been more about ideas. It works really well together. I love dreaming about the possibilities of materials and all the things you can do with them.

Where do you get your craft inspiration?

H: I've got quite a lovely collection of charity-shop-stroke-boot-fair craft books. You know; three kings made out of toilet rolls, that kind of stuff. In our next collection there's some macramé, so we've been looking at cool, old macramé books that have pictures of bearded men wearing helmets made of macramé! I've got an old macramé owl I found 10 years ago that I made into a necklace – it's as big as my entire torso and I just wear it. There have been times when I've taken an embroidery hoop, with embroidery on it and the needle still in it, and I've made it into a necklace. Just a normal thing!

R: We use the internet for images too, and we go to the British Library. I get ideas when I'm out on my bike, or seeing bits of film or theatre or art galleries or gigs or parties, book launches – it's all of it. I just became a member of the Artworkers Guild, and that's so inspiring. William Morris was a member. There was a lecture the other week about the colour orange in painting from 1450 to 1500. Also, pop culture is a massive influence. Subcultures are a massive influence. Our friends. Conversation is the most inspiring thing really. It takes you on different journeys to different endings.

Do you feel part of a craft movement?

R: Definitely. Sometimes I feel, in a personal way - as Rosie, not as Tatty Devine - a bit periphery, a bit "been there, done that". But I still love making stuff; it's still so much part of my life. I make stuff all the time, for myself, and that will never change, whether it's trendy or not. I think that as a woman I've proved a lot through Tatty Devine and I don't need to prove anything through subverting craft - I just genuinely love skill. Learning how to do stuff is a brilliant thing and we're planning more workshops to communicate what we do and how to do it.

H: I really think it's great that people want to make stuff. Sometimes people think that what we do is really expensive - because it takes ages and we make it my hand, here in this country - but if people want to make it themselves, I say, "Make it yourself." Absolutely. It's nice to know that there's a community of people out there who appreciate making things as well. And it was really cool when we first started going to Cast Off [knitting club], about 10 years ago. It was really fun.

R: We knitted on stage at a Chicks on Speed gig. It was quite hardcore, and people thought it was all really freaky. Now it's just another signal of being hip, and there are elements of tweeness to the craft scene, but I think that's all positive. It's gone in a direction that's really accessible.

What is your dream craft project?

R: My immediate thought is to have a derelict house that I could make everything for - down to making the carpets. My granny actually recreated a Roman mosaic floor in a cross-stitch carpet. Quite amazing. I was looking at it the other day in awe. That was probably her lifetime's work. Imagine; she did it square by square. I'd like to take that and push it further - find the ultimate pixilated image and recreate it. That could be very cool. I love cross-stitch. If you're looking at a computer all day and night, you're thinking in pixels anyway, and you've got it really. It's quite simple.

Tatty Devine's
Mega Ping-Pong Hair Bobble

By Rosie Wolfenden and Harriet Vine

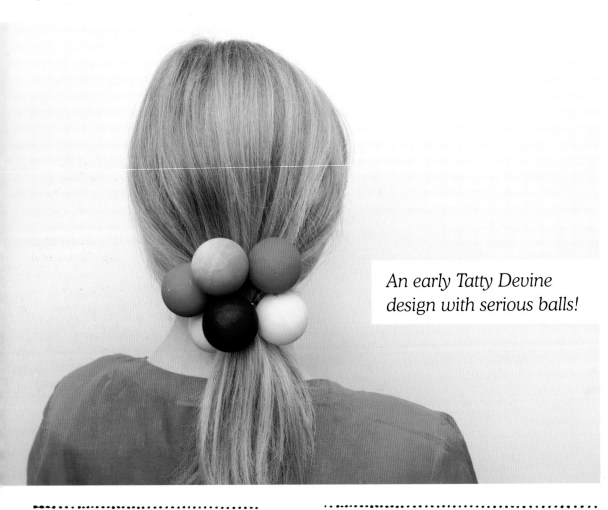

An early Tatty Devine design with serious balls!

Tools

~ scissors
~ marker pen
~ short length of fishing line
~ hand drill with a 3mm bit
~ crimper, or flat-nose pliers
  (optional)

Materials

~ six-pack of ping-pong balls – snazzy
  colours are fun, but white ones would
  work just as well
~ approx 50cm of 2mm round elastic
~ crimp, or small metal tube approx
  6mm wide (optional)

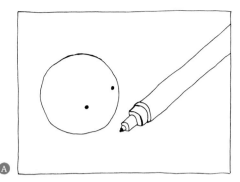

A

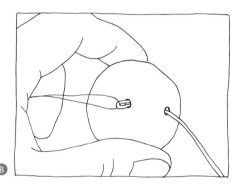

B

What to do

1. Mark where you are going to drill into the first ball; two points about 1.5cm apart (fig A). Drill into the ping-pong ball at the marks. Repeat for all six balls.
2. Double over a length of fishing line and thread the looped end into one of the holes, keeping hold of the ends. Thread the elastic into the other hole, making sure it goes through the loop inside the ball. Pull out the fishing line and the end of the elastic should come with it (fig B).
3. Thread on half the ping-pong balls, followed by the crimp tube if you have one.
4. Add the rest of the ping-pong balls.
5. Thread the two ends of elastic through opposite ends of the crimp tube and adjust the length so both sides are equal. Squeeze the tube tightly with crimper or pliers. If you are knotting, tie two overhand knots with each end by making a loop around the long length and pulling the ends through so all the strands of elastic are fastened together; then tie the two ends together for good measure.
6. Cut off the ends of elastic close to the crimp or the knot.

TIP
To give your hair the Jim Henderson treatment, thread two white ping-pong balls onto a bobble and draw cartoon eyes on them.

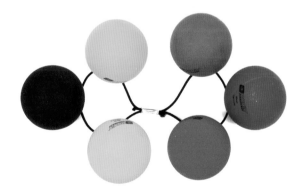

Harriet Vine and Rosie Wolfenden are the design force behind Tatty Devine, the cult, offbeat jewellery brand they started 10 years ago that is now widely recognised for its signature acrylic silhouette shapes – from dinosaurs to chip forks to trapeze artists. The pieces are sold in their two London boutiques and at over 100 stockists worldwide, while their custom-made name necklaces have been worn by countless celebs. *www.tattydevine.com*.

House of Ismay's **Hard-Backed Book**

By Sarah Pounder

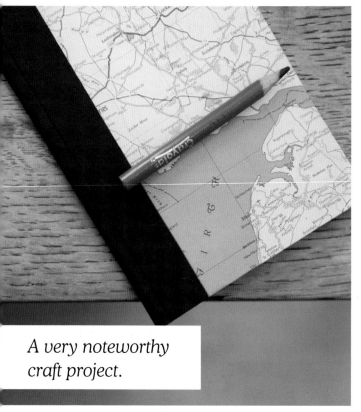

A very noteworthy craft project.

Tools

~ binder's needle
~ awl (or a needle with the blunt end pushed into a cork)
~ bone folder (optional)
~ shoe knife
~ scalpel
~ cutting mat
~ metal ruler
~ scissors
~ large glue brush (a pastry brush is ideal)

Materials

~ six sheets of plain A4 paper
~ one sheet of coloured A4 paper
~ patterned paper for the cover*
~ bookcloth*
~ greyboard or 1mm-thick card*
~ PVA glue
~ linen thread
~ mull (or a piece of lightweight, loosely woven cotton will do)*
~ scrap paper
~ greaseproof paper

* These instructions are for an A6 book, but you can make any size of book by adjusting the measurements

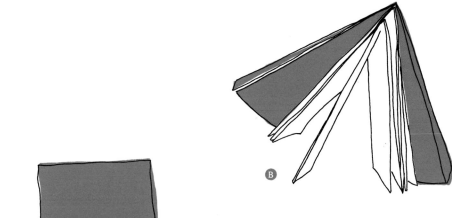

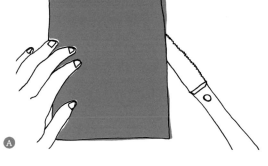

What to do

1. First of all, you need to check the grain of your paper and greyboard. Paper has a grain just like wood does, and it must always run in the same direction as the spine of the book. If the grain runs across the book and picks up any moisture from the air, the paper will expand slightly and the book will warp. A4 printer paper will nearly always have the grain running down the length of the sheet. If you gently bend the paper down the middle lengthways, you will find it gives a lot less resistance than if you bend it in half crossways. You may even be able to see the direction of the grain in the greyboard as it will have little flecks and fibres running in the same direction, but bending it is generally the best way to check.

2. Fold a sheet of paper in half from top to bottom and rub along the crease with the bone folder to make it crisp (every fold you make should be made this way but if you don't have a bone folder just use your thumbnail).

3. Use the shoe knife to gently slice the crease to just past halfway (fig A). Fold the sheet in half again, from top to bottom, to make an A6 booklet.

4. Repeat steps 2 and 3 for each sheet of plain and coloured paper. Then tuck each booklet into the centre of the next, ending with the coloured paper on the outside (fig B).

5. From a piece of scrap paper, cut a strip approx 40mm wide and the same length as the folded side of your book (this should be about 148mm). Make a fold down the length of this strip and use a pencil and ruler to make five evenly spaced marks along the inside of the crease. This will be your guide for making the sewing holes.

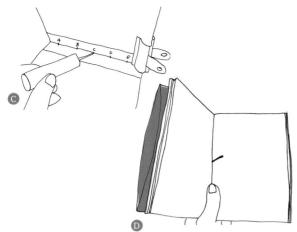

6. Tap the stack of pages together so they are all lined up neatly and hold them together with the guide in the centre. You might want to hold half the pages together with a bulldog clip or a peg. Open up the booklet and using the awl, make a hole through the papers where each mark is (fig C), then remove the guide.

7. Cut a piece of mull 120mm x 50mm. Fold this in half lengthways and place round the coloured paper over the holes you have just made.

8. Now you are ready to stitch the papers together with strong linen thread (if you want more decorative stitches you can use coloured silk thread). Your thread will need to be twice the length of the book plus enough extra to tie the final knot. The easiest way to explain the sewing method is to assign each hole with a letter starting with A nearest the top of the book and going down to E at the bottom. Start with the needle outside the book and pass the thread through the centre hole, or C (fig D). Make sure to leave enough thread sticking out to tie the final knot with. Then you just have to pass the thread through the holes in this order – out through B, in A, out B, in D, out E, in D.

9. The final stitch should go out through C again, but make sure that the two loose ends of thread are either side of the stitch you made going from B to D. Pull the stitches tight, tie a double knot (fig E) and then trim the loose threads.

10. Using a metal ruler and a scalpel, trim the foredge of the book (the edge opposite the spine). You just need to tidy up the edges. Measure out an equal distance across the top and bottom of your book to make sure that the foredge is perfectly parallel with the spine. Hold the ruler firmly, then carefully slice through the book block (fig F); it may take a few cuts. Do the same with top and bottom edges for a neat booklet. Press it under a weight or a heavy book to keep it flat.

11. To make the cover, cut two rectangles of the greyboard, making sure that the grain runs down lengthways; the size depend on the measurements of your finished book block. They should be 6mm longer than the book and 3mm narrower. Position the boards either side of the book, 6mm in from the spine, so that 3mm of card sticks out from the top, bottom and foredge (fig G).

12. The length of your bookcloth should be the length of the book plus a 20mm overlap at the top and bottom (so add 40mm). To work out how wide it should be, measure the distance around the spine from one board to the other. To do this, hold the boards in position with a bulldog clip, wrap a strip of scrap paper around the spine and mark off the back of the boards with a pencil (fig H).

13. Measure this distance and add 40mm; this is the width to cut your bookcloth. Mark 20mm in from the spine on both cover boards (fig I). This will help you to position the cloth.

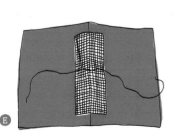

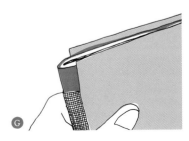

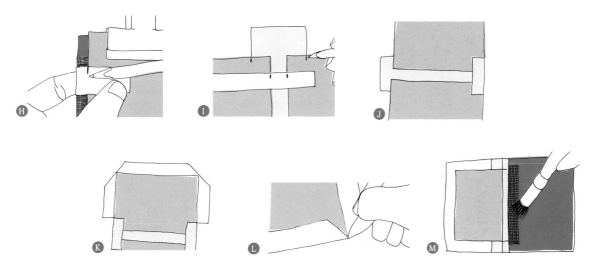

14. Cover the book cloth in a layer of glue and lay down flat, glue up. Position the boards on the cloth lining up the 20mm markers. At the ends, fold the overlapping fabric round the boards (fig J). Use the bone folder to rub the cloth down, making sure it is stuck firmly with no creases or bubbles.

15. Cut two pieces of patterned paper for the covers so that you have a 20mm overlap at each edge of the greyboard and 1mm-2mm to overlap the bookcloth. Glue one piece of paper and lay it down flat, glue up! Lay the greyboard on top so that the paper is covering 1mm-2mm of the bookcloth, then press down. Cut a triangle off each corner, 1mm-2mm out from the corner of the boards (fig K).

16. Fold the long edge over and rub down with the bone folder. Use the pointed end of your bone folder to tuck the paper in neatly at the corner (fig L), then fold the short edges over. Rub along all edges to make sure the paper is well stuck down. Leave to dry, and then cover the other greyboard in the same way.

17. Place a piece of scrap paper under the first end paper to protect the rest of the pages, then cover this first page in glue, sticking the mull down as you do so (fig M). Remove the scrap paper and place the block glue side up in its correct position on the back cover (3mm in from the top, foredge and bottom). Carefully, holding the block in place by the foredge, fold the front cover over the glued side of the book and press down gently. Turn the book over, open the back cover and repeat the gluing process.

18. Gently open the covers slightly to check there are no wrinkles in the end papers. If there are, you can smooth them out with the bone folder, but you shouldn't open the book too much until it has dried. Place a piece of greaseproof paper in between the end papers to prevent any glue seeping out and ruining the book, and press the book under a weight until it is dry.

Sarah Pounder works from her home in rural Suffolk, creating books, cards and jewellery out of vintage paper and leather. When she's not in her studio, she is out visiting friends, walking along riverbanks, or at boot fairs looking for more exciting things to recycle or clutter up her house with. *www.houseofismay.com, www.etsy.com/shop/ismay.*

Janine Basil's **Superstar Fascinator**

To wear to weddings, on nights out or just when you fancy a bit of fun in your day.

Tools
- ~ dressmakers' pins
- ~ large needle
- ~ marker pen
- ~ thimble
- ~ tape measure
- ~ scissors
- ~ elastic band
- ~ clingfilm
- ~ paper
- ~ spray bottle filled with water
- ~ large mixing bowl, or another rounded object to act as your block
- ~ old pillowcase or large scrap of cotton fabric

Materials
- ~ approx 25cm x 25cm of buckram
- ~ two squares of felt in the colour of your fascinator,
- ~ all-purpose glue
- ~ 45cm of hat elastic
- ~ sewing thread to match the felt
- ~ rhinestones (and Gem-Tac glue), buttons, ribbons or anything to decorate that you fancy!

What to do

1. Start by covering your "block" (mixing bowl) with the fabric, and tie at the bottom with an elastic band. Then cover this in clingfilm. You may need to pin this to the fabric. Keep an area at least 15cm in diameter as free of creases as possible – you can use pins to hold some of the creases back.

2. Cut two squares from the buckram, about 15cm x 15cm, making sure the grain of the buckram is as straight as possible. Spray lightly with water on both sides and leave for a few moments; you'll find the buckram gets very soft and pliable. Place both pieces, one on top of the other, on your prepared round surface and pin the top edge onto the fabric. Then, gently pull the bottom edge down so it starts to take on the curve of the surface; pin this down. Repeat with the sides, and then the corners – on the corners you'll need to pull a little harder to bring the buckram in snug against the surface. Pin down (fig A). Leave to dry for at least 24 hours.

3. Meanwhile, draw a star on paper and cut out. Play around with sizes, placing the stars against your head until you're happy with the result.

4. Once dry, remove the buckram from the block and place the paper star on it. Draw around the template with the marker pen – this is a little fiddly as you're working on a curved surface. Just mark all the corners then join them up. Cut out.

5. Cover the entire top side with glue, making sure it's not too thick. Leave this for a few moments to go slightly tacky, then place a square of felt on it and press down. You may need to very gently stretch the felt so it fits the curves. Leave to dry for about 20 minutes. Turn it over and trim the edges, leaving about 1mm-2mm of felt over the edge of the buckram (fig B).

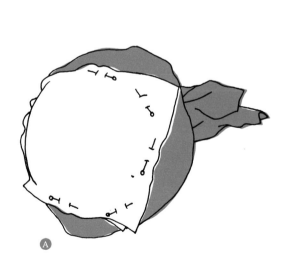

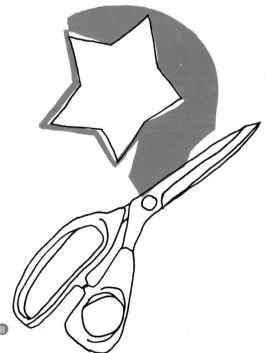

6. Cut a piece of the elastic to 45cm, tie a small knot in either end and sew one end onto either side of the fascinator. Use your thimble as the buckram can be a little tough to get through. Make small stitches from the wrong side to the right side of the fascinator and sew over the elastic (not through it). Put it on your head to check the length of the elastic. If it needs to be shortened, simply pull the elastic through and make a new knot.

7. Here's the fun bit: decorating! You can sew or glue on whatever you fancy – buttons, rhinestones, maybe some glitter fabric and ribbon. Go to town. For a bit of sparkle, glue on loads of rhinestones, one by one, with Gem-Tac glue. (If you are sewing anything on, make sure you use the thimble).

8. To attach the lining, cover the bottom with glue as you did with the top side, making sure you cover the elastic, as this will help to hold it firm. Place the lining felt on the glued side and smooth into the curve. Make sure the edges are all stuck firmly. Allow to dry.

9. From the top side, trim the excess felt from the lining, avoiding the elastic. Put on your glad rags, pop on your fascinator and wow them all!

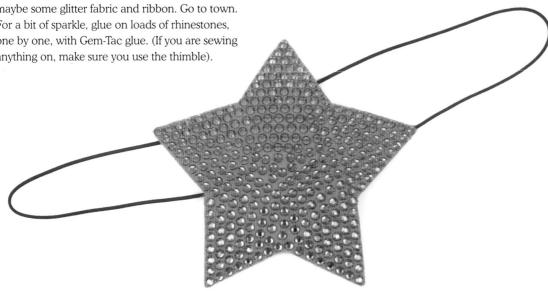

"There's a certain amount of flexibility in this project. Size and decoration are all up to your imagination. Get started making a whole host of gorgeous headpieces – it's addictive!"

Janine Basil has been involved in fashion, fabrics and making in various ways for most of her life. Millinery has always bubbled under the surface but now it's the focus of her passion. Based in north-west London, the inspirations for her hats and fascinators range from vintage designs to comic books to burlesque, and when she's not watching old movies or playing computer games, she creates new items in her downtime too. *www.janinebasil.com.*

Wooden Tree's
Wonderfully Woolly Mobile

By Kirsty Anderson

Look to the clouds and mountains wherever you live!

Tools
~ dressmakers' pins
~ sewing needle
~ scraps of paper
~ pliers
~ wire cutters
~ extra pair of helping hands for the tricky bits!
~ sewing machine (optional)

Materials
~ woolly mountain-coloured jumper (felted in the wash at 60°)
~ small bag of toy stuffing
~ felt squares in various shades: white, blue, grey
~ approx 1m of soft, thin cotton fabric
~ three metal coat hangers
~ 0.5m strip of cream or white lace
~ sewing thread
~ strong white thread, such as topstitch
~ string
~ sticky tape

What to do

Woolly mountain

1. Draw two triangle templates on paper, 14cm and 10cm high.
2. Turn the felted jumper inside out. Place and pin templates onto the best patterned bits of the jumper.
3. Cut around the templates through both layers of the jumper, 1cm from the edge for seam allowance (fig A). Cut out two big and three small mountains.

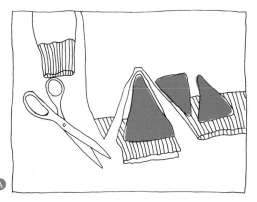

4. Un-pin the paper, open up the two pieces of triangle, and place a small piece of lace at the top of one triangle (fig B) – this will be the snowy peak. Place the triangles back on top of one another, with the lace sandwiched in the middle, and the jumper pieces still inside out (right sides facing); then pin.

5. Stitch around the triangle 1cm from the edge using a running stitch (or a straight stitch on a sewing machine), leaving a 4cm gap along one side (fig C). Snip the extra wool away from the corners (but not too close to the stitching). Gently but firmly turn the mountain right side out.

6. Stuff using a pencil, paintbrush etc, then hand-sew the gap closed with a whipstitch.
7. Repeat steps 4-6 for all the mountains.

Felt clouds – like the mountains, but a bit different!

1. Draw various cloud templates, around 10cm wide, on paper.
2. Pin a template to two layers of felt and cut around it 0.5cm from the edge.
3. Stitch around the cloud shape – again, with a running stitch or a sewing machine – 0.5cm in from the edge and leaving a 3cm gap for stuffing (do not turn inside out though).
4. Stuff using a pencil, paintbrush etc and hand-sew the gap closed with a running stitch that joins up with the edge stitching (fig D).
6. Make as many clouds as you like, in various shapes and sizes, and decorate them with stitches of rain, sun, felt birds etc.

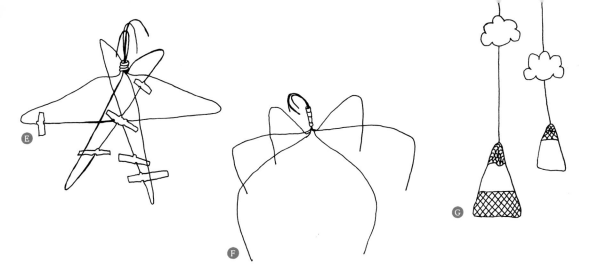

Coat hanger frame

1. Overlap the coat hangers so they make an upright star shape (fig E). Hold them together with string at the top, and position the wire on the floor with even spaces between them – tape the bottom to the ground to help position them.
2. Discard the string and secure the neck tightly with sticky tape.
3. Using pliers, turn the hooks at the top so they are all facing one way, forming one solid hook or loop.
4. Using wire cutters, cut through the straight wires at the bottom of all the hangers at the centre point: here you may need a helping hand.
5. Stretch the wire out so the metal ends point to the ground, using the pliers to round the corners of the hanger (fig F). Cut the ends to even up the lengths of wire and to create your desired shape.
7. Cut 1cm-wide strips of thin cotton fabric and wrap them around all parts of the hanger, covering the metal.
8. Use glue, or a needle and thread, to secure any loose bits of fabric.

The mobile

1. Now you need to assemble all the parts together. Take the stronger thread, and cut several lengths measuring roughly between 20cm and 70cm.
3. Tie a secure knot at the end of the thread, then use a needle to stitch it onto the top middle of a cloud or mountain.
4. If you want to add a cloud further up the thread, push the needle into the bottom of the cloud and through to the top, pulling through a length of thread long enough to attach to the mobile. At the top of the cloud, secure the thread with a couple of stitches (fig G).
5. Remember, the mobile needs to balance, so be generally even with your placement of clouds and mountains. Attach the threads to the ends of the hanger. Use sticky tape to try out different positions and heights until you are happy, then tie the threads firmly to the coat hangers.
Phew. Done!

Kirsty Anderson nests in Edinburgh where she creates plush accessories and art using the Scottish woodlands as inspiration and her granny's linen closet for materials. She likes to recycle as much as she can, making new memories from old ones. Mostly she likes to stitch, rummage in thrift shops, wander the woods and show people how to make silly things like floral shark oven-gloves. *www.wooden-tree.blogspot.com, www.awoodentree.etsy.com.*

Knit and Destroy's **Paintbrush Scarf**

By Kandy Diamond

Stay warm 'n' cosy while expressing the artist in you!

Tools

~ pair of 3.25mm knitting needles
~ yarn needle

Materials

~ 4-ply wool yarn in 50g balls (such as Rowan pure wool 4-ply) in the following colours and quantities:
   ~ A Black (black 404) – two balls
   ~ B Grey (shale 402) – one ball
   ~ C Beige (toffee 453) – one ball
   ~ D Paint colour (kiss 436) – one ball

Knit skills

~ cast on
~ knit, purl and rib
~ increase/decrease
~ slip stitch

What to do

1. Using yarn A, cast on 18 sts.
2. The pattern is worked in a knit-1-purl-1 rib throughout, with the first stitches "slipped" for neat edge. First, shape the brush handle as follows:
   Row 1: k1, p1 to end.
   Row 2: sl1, *p1, k1; rep from * to last st, p1.
   Rows 3-9: as row 2.
   Row 10 (first increase row): m1 (p1, k1 into one stitch – purl into the front and knit into the back), *p1, k1; rep from * to last st, m1 (p1, k1 – as before). You have 20 sts.
   Row 11: sl1, *k1, p1; rep from * to last st, k1.
   Rows 12-19: as row 11.
   Row 20 (second increase row): m1 (k1, p1 – knit into the front and purl into the back), *k1, p1; rep from * to last st, m1 (k1, p1 – as before). You now have 22 sts.
   Row 21: sl1, *p1, k1; rep from * to last st, p1.
   Rows 22-29: as row 21. Repeat rows 10-29 five more times. You will now have 42 sts.
3. Add length:
   Continue working in k1-p1 rib (sl1, *p1, k1; rep from * to last stitch, p1) until work measures 135cm.
4. Shape the metal tip:
   Switch to yarn B. You will be working in colour B for the next 40 rows, with the exception of 2 single-row stripes of colour A at rows 5 and 10.
   Rows 1-3: sl1,*p1, k1; rep from * to last st, p1.
   Row 4 (first decrease row): p2tog,*k1, p1; rep from * to last 2 sts, k2tog. You now have 40 sts.
   Row 5: join in A. P1, k1 to end.
   Row 6: using B. P1, k1 to end.
   Row 7: sl1, *k1, p1; rep from * to last stitch, k1.
   Row 8 (decrease row): k2tog, *p1 k1; rep from * to last 2 sts, p2tog.
   Row 9: sl1, *p1, k1; rep from * to last st, p1.
   Row 10: using A. K1, p1 to end.
   Row 11: using B. K1, p1 to end.
   Row 12 (decrease row): p2tog, *k1, p1; rep from * to last 2 sts, k2tog.
   Rows 13-15: sl1, *k1, p1; rep from * to last st, k1.
   Row 16 (decrease row): k2tog, *p1, k1; rep from * to last 2 sts, p2tog. You now have 34 sts.
   Rows 17-19: sl1, *p1, k1; rep from * to last st, p1.
   Repeat rows 12-19 twice more. You will now have 26 sts.
   Row 36 (decrease): p2tog, *k1, p1; rep from * to last 2 sts, k2tog.
   Rows 37-39: sl1, *k1, p1; rep from * to last st, k1.
   Row 40 (decrease): k2tog, *p1, k1; rep from * to last 2 sts, p2tog. You will now have 22 sts
   Row 41: join in A. K1, p1 to end.
5. Shape the bristles:
   Row 42: join in C. K1, p1 to end.
   Row 43 (increase row): m1 (p1, k1 into one stitch – purl into the front and knit into the back), *p1, k1; rep from * to last st, m1 (p1, k1 – as before).
   Row 44: sl1, *k1, p1; rep from * to last st, k1.
   Row 45 (increase row): m1 (k1, p1 into one stitch – knit into the front and purl into the back), *k1, p1; rep from * to last st, m1 (k1, p1 – as before).
   Row 46: sl1, *p1, k1; rep from * to last st, p1.
   Repeat rows 43-46 four more times. You will have 42 sts.
   Rows 58-60: sl1, *p1, k1; rep from * to last st, p1.
6. Shape the paint-dip:
   Row 61: join in D. K1, p1 to end.
   Rows 62-64: sl1, *p1, k1; rep from * to last st, p1.
   Row 65 (decrease row): k2tog,*p1,k1; rep from * to last 2 sts, p2tog.
   Row 66 (decrease row): p2tog,*k1, p1; rep from * to last 2 sts, k2tog.
   Repeat rows 65 and 66 until 4 sts are left. Cast off.
7. Hooray! You have knitted yourself an awesome paintbrush scarf. Use the yarn needle to weave the loose yarn ends back into the body of the scarf.

Kandy Diamond is the brains and brawn behind Knit and Destroy: the one-woman knit machine that makes a range of fun, novelty and top-quality knits. When she isn't knitting, or roller-skating around and drinking gallons of tea, Kandy is a keen all round crafter and co-writes the biannual craft zine *Sugar Paper: 20 things to make and do*. *www.knitanddestroy.co.uk*, *www.sugarpapergang.blogspot.com*.

The Cat in the Shoe's
Curious Time-Keeping Cushion

By Lucy Brasher

Make sure you're not late for a very important date…

Tools

- dressmakers' pins
- sewing needle
- paintbrush
- tailors' chalk, or pencil
- scissors
- ruler
- set of compasses
- sewing machine (optional)

Materials

- approx 40cm x 40cm of canvas or cream cotton fabric
- approx 55cm x 40cm of a fabric of your choice for the clock back
- approx 30cm x 15cm of a stripy fabric
- felt in a colour of your choice for the numbers and hands
- gold fabric paint
- stuffing
- sewing thread in black and white

What to do

1. Firstly, cut out all the elements. Using the set of compasses, draw a circle of 35cm diameter onto the canvas. Cut around the circle about 1cm outside the line. This is the clock face.
2. Cut a circle the same size from the fabric you have selected for the clock back. On another piece of the same fabric, draw two rectangles measuring 6cm x 5cm. Cut out 1cm from the line.
3. For the clock winder, draw two circles of 10cm diameter on the stripy fabric. Again, cut out 1cm from the line. On both circles, use a ruler to straighten the bottom edge, ensuring the stripe is horizontal.
4. Using a computer, type numbers 1 to 12 in bold Times font, 150pt. (You can use whatever font you like, but this size works well.) Print and cut out the numbers. Draw around the 3, 6, 9 and 12 in chalk on the felt. Cut them out along with two strips, approx 15cm and 11cm in length, for the clock hands.
5. Draw a circle of 32cm diameter on a piece of paper. Cut this out on the line.
6. Place the paper circle in the centre of the canvas circle and draw around it in pencil (don't worry, the line will get covered). Now, with your fabric paint, paint from the fabric edge to this drawn line, creating a border.
7. While this is drying, make the winder for your clock from the two rectangles and two stripy circles. Place the rectangles together with the right sides of the fabric facing each other. Sew together 1cm in from the edge leaving one short end open so you can turn it right side out.
8. Do the same with the circles, leaving the straight end open. Turn both shapes right side out and stuff them.
9. Hand-sew the bottom of the rectangle closed; it doesn't matter what it looks like, as now you need to trap this end inside the gap in the stripy circle. Pin in place. Sew the two sections together neatly, with a whipstitch, so you have what looks a bit like a mushroom. Make sure the rough edge of the stripy fabric is turned under.
10. Once the clock face is dry, add the numbers. Carefully position the felt ones, making sure they are evenly spaced, and pin on the remaining paper numbers. Sew on the felt with a running stitch around the edge of each figure. Sew around the paper numbers on the canvas with a backstitch.
11. Next, attach the clock hands in the centre. Make a good strong knot in the black thread, sew through both hands, so that the knot is at the front, and into the canvas, where you need to make another firm knot. Don't pull the thread too tight, as you want to be able to move the hands.
12. Now all you need to do is put it all together... Place the watch back and front together, right sides facing each other, and pin. Sew the circles together 1cm in from the edge, leaving a gap at the top between numbers 11 and 1. Turn right side round and stuff to your hearts content.
13. Finally, pin the fancy mushroom-looking winder in the centre of the gap at the top of the clock. Hand-sew the gap closed and the winder in place, making sure to fold in the rough fabric edges neatly.

"Have a good old-fashioned lie down and rest your head on your masterpiece!"

Lucy Brasher is a creator and maker of handmade creatures and curiosities (such as pie girls and monsters) residing in Bournmouth, on the south coast of England, with her fella, possessed cat, scrumptious son and a ridiculous amount of books, sewing machines and unmade ideas. *www.thecatintheshoe.com, www.etsy.com/shop/thecatintheshoe.*

Louise Kamara's and Elizabeth Cake's
Reclaimed Clothing Lampshade

*Lighting the way,
vintage-eco style.*

Tools
~ scissors
~ ruler
~ measuring tape
~ stiff plastic "tucking stick" made
from an old credit card or similar

Materials
~ any lightweight woven fabric
that lies flat and has a seam-free
area of at least 75cm x 22cm –
old clothing, curtains etc
~ an old straight-sided lampshade
frame that has two rings the
same size
~ approx 2m of 1cm-wide double-
sided sticky tape
~ approx 1m x 22cm of 200gsm or
similar lightweight cardboard
~ glue such as PVA, fabric glue or
spray mount

What to do

1. Measure around the circumference of one of the rings.

2. Add 1cm to this measurement (to allow for overlap), and mark out this length on the cardboard. This is the long length of the rectangle that makes up the shade. The short side of the rectangle is the drop of the shade and should measure between 20cm and 30cm, depending on how long you'd like the finished shade to be. Draw a rectangle to these measurements and cut out.

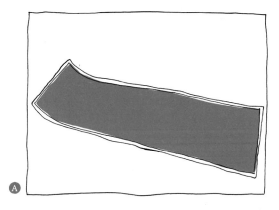

Ⓐ

3. Place the cardboard on the wrong side of the fabric, following the grain.

4. Glue the card onto the fabric and cut out your shade shape, leaving 1cm of fabric either side of the long edges (fig A).

5. Cut two lengths of double-sided adhesive tape to the measurement of the ring circumference. Remove the covering strip from one side of the tape and lay this along the edge of the ring, rolling it around the steel. Repeat for the second ring. Lay another strip of tape along one short length of the shade shape and then remove the all the backing tape.

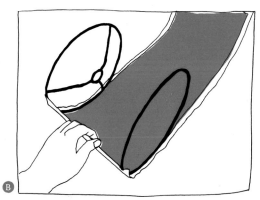

Ⓑ

6. Position the rings at the edges of the cardboard and roll the rings carefully along the cardboard edges at the top and bottom long lengths (fig B).

7. Seal the overlap at the short edge, pressing the sticky-taped side on top of the other edge.

8. Using a triangle of plastic, tuck the raw edges of fabric underneath the inside of the ring (fig C), snipping the fabric around the gimble supports that run into the centre of the frame. Your shade is now ready to use – with a low-energy bulb, naturally!

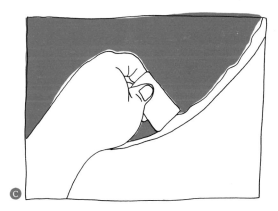

Ⓒ

Louise Kamara lives in London and runs sustainable design events and workshops, including the Eco Design Fair and the Vintage Festival, encouraging people to intercept items going to landfill and do something more more beautiful, more useful with them. *www.ecodesignfair. co.uk, www.vintagebyhemingway.co.uk*.
Elizabeth Cake has been commissioned to make lampshades out of everything from old clothing to a much-loved candlewick bedspread. She also runs lampshade-making workshops. *www.midnightbell-lampshades.com*.

Lou Rota's **Decoupage Chair**

The ubiquitous is transformed into something unique.

Tools

~ a couple of medium-sized paintbrushes
~ sandpaper in coarse and fine grades
~ scissors

Materials

~ polypropylene stacking chair
~ lots of seed catalogues and gardening magazines
~ decoupage medium; Applicraft make a good one, or you can use diluted PVA
~ 0.5l tin of water-based varnish, such as Polyvine high-gloss lacquer
~ dead-flat acrylic varnish, such as Polyvine Dead-Flat Decorators Varnish

What to do

1. First, you need to give your chair a thorough sanding all over to give the lacquer a good base to stick to. Start with rougher sandpaper, and then a fine one. Don't forget to do around the edges of the underside too; you want the paper to stick very well here.
2. Dilute a small amount of the varnish with water, and paint over the plastic. Apply a second undiluted coat and leave to dry.
3. Cut out *lots* of flowers – some in their entirety, and with others just cut around half the flower, leaving the rest of the background in situ. Make sure you've got a nice big collection before you start on the chair.

4. Practise laying out the flowers. The trick is to make the flowers look seamless. Overlap each flower over a section of background (as opposed to overlapping flowers over each other). Try to match similarly coloured backgrounds, then cover over any joins with individual cut-out flowers.
5. Apply the flowers to the chair, starting at the edges and working inwards; brush glue onto the back of the paper and then, working reasonably quickly, stick it onto the chair. Use the brush and a little more glue on the top to smooth out any bumps or air bubbles, working from the centre outwards. Wait for one area to dry before applying another layer.
6. To get round corners you have to cut along one edge of the paper with lots of parallel snips a few millimetres apart, then glue and wrap each frond around the corner one at a time, helping it on its way with a little glue on your brush. This takes time, but is very satisfying. Once it is completely covered – which could take several days – let it dry overnight.
7. Now, it needs several coats of varnish; 10 to 12 if you can. Use the lacquer you started with again, with a very, very light sanding in between (if you still have the patience). The more coats it has, the more robust it will be and the better it will look. If you prefer a matt finish, use the dead-flat acrylic varnish for the last two coats.

> **TIP**
> **Not feeling floral? Use the same technique with old comics, newspaper, maps, sheet music or any other paper you can find.**

Lou Rota produces a selection of decorative, upcycled ceramics and furniture. She also makes a range of handmade English bone china tableware and mugs featuring her trademark bugs and birds, as well as designing a manufactured collection for Anthropologie. Lou works from a garden studio in north-west London, where she lives with her husband, Gavin, and daughters, Rosie and Ava. *www.lourota.com*.

Dot your T's and Cross your I's
Pom-Pom Brooch & Necklace

By Chloe Bosher

A chic vintage-scarf take on this crafty, fluffy ball.

Tools
~ sewing needle
~ set of compasses
~ scissors
~ flat-nose pliers, or tweezers

Materials
~ vintage square scarf (in georgette, chiffon, silk or any fabric that would give a frayed-edge look. The one used here measured 88cm x 88cm)
~ 1m of 0.5cm-thick ribbon
~ three sieve brooch pin backs (found at most bead shops)
~ sewing thread
~ small pieces of cardboard, such as from a cereal packet
~ approx 50cm of braid or rope for the necklace
~ all-purpose glue
~ pair of bell closers with clasp to fit the width of the braid

What to do

Pom-pom brooch

1. Draw two circles of 6cm diameter on the cardboard. Then draw another circle of 2cm diameter in the centre. Cut around the circumference of the circles and remove the middle to create a doughnut shape.
2. Cut the vintage scarf into strips approximately 2cm wide.
3. Place the two cardboard circles together and tie the first strip around the cardboard ring to secure. Now begin wrapping the strip around the circle going through the hole in the centre each time and covering the cardboard as you go around the circle (fig A). To add the next strip, overlap the fabric slightly over the last wrap, securing both ends.
4. Continue wrapping the strips of fabric around the circle until the middle of the ring is full and you cannot pass any more fabric through the hole (fig B).

5. Now start cutting through the individual fabric loops around the outside edge of the circle. To keep the pom-pom together as you go around it helps to place a cup on top of the circle. Cut through all the layers until you reach the cardboard inside, wiggling the scissors between the two pieces of cardboard to cut the last layer.
6. Once every loop is cut, separate the two cardboard rings slightly and tie a strip of ribbon tightly around the centre. Tear away the cardboard rings to reveal the pom-pom. Fluff up! Cut away any loose strands or frayed edges.
7. Attach one side of the pom-pom to the sieve part of the brooch back by gathering some of the strands together and sewing them to the sieve.
8. Attach the clasp part of brooch back to the sieve by bending the four clips around the edge of the sieve using a pair of flat-nose pliers or tweezers.

Pom-pom necklace

1. Make three pom-pom brooches following steps 1-8 above.
2. Cut a strip of braid to your desired necklace length. Put some glue inside the base of both ends of the bell closers, then insert one end of the braid into each (fig C) and leave to dry overnight. Putting it in the fridge will help the glue to set.
3. Pin each of the brooches to the braid in a suitable arrangement.

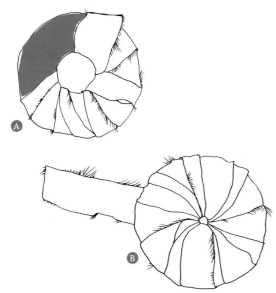

Chloe Bosher is a fashion graduate turned accessories designer. Her brand, Dot your T's and Cross your I's, introduces a playful theme to everyday outfits with pom-pom hairbands, brooches and necklaces, and semi-precious stone jewellery. She uses bold fabrics such as silk and vintage scarves as well as leather in more recent designs. Follow her pom-pom journey at *www.dotyourteas.com* and *www.dotyourteas.blogspot.com*.

Love From Hetty & Dave's
Bunny-Heart Brooch

By Zoe Larkins

Wear your heart on your sleeve – or rather your lapel – with a brooch full of hand-stitched charm.

Tools
~ small leather needle
~ scissors
~ leather hole punch, or seed beads

Materials
~ piece of cardboard from a cereal box or similar
~ 10cm x 20cm of red leather
~ 10cm x 10cm of white leather
~ small scrap of peach/pink leather or felt for rabbit nose and ears
~ brooch back pin
~ approx 50cm of stripy ribbon
~ polyester toy stuffing
~ all-purpose glue
~ sewing thread in white and black

(A)

(B)

(C)

TIP
e-Bay is a great source for leather scraps.

What to do

1. Draw a heart approx 8cm across on the piece of card. Cut out and draw around it. Inside this second heart, draw a slightly smaller heart with a frilly edge and another heart about 1cm-1.5cm inside this (fig A). Cut out the frilly heart and its inner heart.

2. On the red leather, draw around the plain heart template twice. Draw around the frilly heart on the white leather. Draw a rabbit face in the middle of the frilly heart. Cut everything out.

3. Punch holes all around the frill, or stitch on tiny seed beads if you don't have a leather punch.

4. Glue the white frilly heart onto the red heart. With white thread, sew a running stitch around the inside of the white heart, attaching it to the red leather.

5. Glue the bunny in the middle, adding a little pink heart-shaped nose and inner ear details in the pink leather. Sew on all the elements with evenly spaced overhand stitches. Don't forget its tiny black eyes: sew two stitches in a small cross for each eye.

6. Cut a 10cm length of ribbon and thread it through the brooch back until the two ends match up. Spread glue onto one half of the back of the ribbon, then stick the other half to it, trapping the brooch back at the top. Make a bow from the remainder of the ribbon (fig B), and stitch it in front of the brooch back.

7. Sandwich the ribbon at the top of the two red hearts (fig C), with the bow and the bunny facing upwards. Glue the hearts together along the edges only, leaving a 4cm or so gap on one side.

8. Stitch around the sides with a whipstitch. When you get to the gap, fill with polyester stuffing, then stitch the gap up.

Zoe Larkins was born on the south coast of England in the late 1970s. Raised on a diet of sequins, buttons, ribbons and thread, it was inevitable that Zoe would develop her first crush on a Singer... After a stint in London, she returned to the seaside and opened a little studio/ shop where she makes and sells all sorts of stitched delights alongside lovely vintage finds. *www.lovefromhettyanddave.co.uk.*

Interview with Mr Wingate's
Sam Wingate

How would you describe the current state of craft? I heard someone use the term "neo-craft" the other day, referring to a new group of people that are making things, but not in a traditional sense. So we're not wood-turners and leather-workers and metalworkers – we are doing something a bit more accessible to everyone, something that requires, perhaps, less of a honed skill. People are using a broader range of skills to make things that are quite pop, rather than traditional.

Is there a tangible craft movement? There are definitely a lot of people making things at the moment, and I think this is being driven by the likes of Etsy and Craft Marketplace. For me personally, I started making things because I wasn't confident enough I could get a job. I went to art school and studied textile design, and just started making things for myself. But I had been making things for myself since I was young. My mum was always telling me to make things myself. I'd say, "Mum, I really want an Etch-A-Sketch." And the answer would be, "Make it yourself." Actually, that was the exception – I had to save up for that one.

What are your earliest crafting memories? I remember making things from scraps of fabric. My mum made us clothes, so I would get really tiny bits of fabric and make purses to put my teeth in. Teeth purses. And one of the earliest products I ever made is still in use in my mum's kitchen – a scissors rack. In my shed there was a box of wood offcuts that I was allowed to use. I laid the scissors on a piece of wood and hammered nails in where they were. That might be the best thing I've ever made!

When did you start making stuff as a business? When I was at art school in Norwich I printed T-shirts for myself. I also had an evening job in a club, where everyone would tell me how nice my T-shirts were and ask where they could buy one. That's when I thought it could be something I made money from, but I didn't actually start doing that until I graduated. Then I moved to London and opened a market stall on Brick Lane so that I could pay the rent on a studio. I did lots of paper stencils and bought five screens, and things built up slowly from there.

Where do you do your craft now? I have a studio in Hackney Wick, right next to the Olympic site. I need enough space to be able to print, and I don't like working at home. Also, it's really nice because there are other people around who I get to share ideas and opportunities with. I also like that it's quiet, especially where I am in Fish Island.

Where do you get your craft inspiration? My work is all illustration, and it's buildings and cities that inspire me. I don't look very far – I take what's around me – and I always make products that I want to use myself. So when I started printing T-shirts it was because that was what I wanted to wear. When I moved into my new flat I wanted homewares, so I did that. It's quite selfish really; I make it for myself then see if I can sell it.

More and more, my process is led by sustainability. I was recently invited to a course on the subject at London College of Fashion, which really made me think about what, as a manufacturer, I waste – and that everything I make is, essentially, waste. So with a cushion, for example, I don't use a zip. You can do quite adequately without one, and it takes something like 200 years to decompose.

What's the best thing you've ever made? Apart from the scissors rack? I'm not really sure. I tend to tire of everything soon after I make them. And because it's printing, I do loads and loads of one design, and so I get sick of it. But there are some things I'm still really proud of, such as the wallpaper I designed for DKNY. That was probably the pinnacle. It's the one that everyone else thinks is good. And I've just started selling in Selfridges, which is really exciting (although they order in really tiny amounts and force your price down), but it's the same products as before.

What's the worst thing you've ever made? There are loads of prints I've done where I've thought, "that would be nice", and then they're horrible. The worst designs tend to be the ones that I think are OK, and then when I show them to people I realise, "What was I thinking." I've got this one hoodie, for example, with a print on the back. I made it when I was trying to beef up my collection and I latched onto an idea that, basically, wasn't very good – boxes leading into other boxes making a kind of machine. It didn't fit with any of my other work, and it just looked stupid. And now I've got this hoodie. I keep thinking about what I can print over it, but I never get round to it.

But I think the worst thing, which still makes me feel a bit sick, was something I made about three years ago. Some friends and I sat around one day printing T-shirts with paper stencils, and I thought it would be really nice to make a stencil of a butterfly, with a face in it. So that's what I did. I didn't realise how horrible it would be until I printed it.

Mr Wingate's **Dazzling 3-D Tee**

By Sam Wingate

Become an optical illusion.

Tools

~ marker pen
~ spoon
~ long metal ruler – at least 60cm long
~ craft knife
~ cutting mat
~ iron
~ approx 50cm x 70cm silkscreen in mesh count 43T – any screen that is sold for use on fabrics in good art shops
~ squeegee (rubber blade) to fit your screen. It needs to be a little shorter than the inside width of the screen
~ a friend to hold the screen when printing is useful too!

Materials

~ white cotton T-shirt.
~ transparent, water-based fabric inks for use on light fabrics (take care not to buy inks for use on dark fabrics) in yellow, light blue and pink
~ four sheets of newsprint or newspaper that are larger than your screen
~ a small piece of cardboard from a cereal box or similar
~ masking tape

What to do

There are two stages to this project: making a stencil and then printing. This is a three-colour print, so you need to make three stencils and print three times.

Making the stencil

1. Copy the template on page 230 onto the piece of card. It should be 8cm x 8cm at its longest points. (If you are using a smaller screen, scale everything down from this point on.) Cut out the template.
2. Draw a square grid in the middle of one of the sheets of newsprint at a diagonal (fig A). Each square should be 9cm x 9cm (or 1cm larger than the shape).
3. Draw lines along the longest lengths of your template to form a cross. Position on the grid, matching up the lines (fig B).
4. Draw around the template and repeat across the grid for three rows across and four rows down (fig C).
5. To cut all three stencils at once, lay two sheets of newsprint under the sheet you just drew on, staggered slightly, and stick the three together with masking tape.
6. Place the papers on the cutting mat. Use the craft knife to cut out all the template shapes.

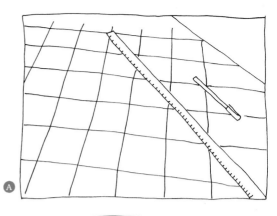

A

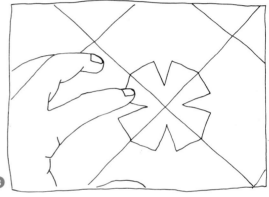

B

C

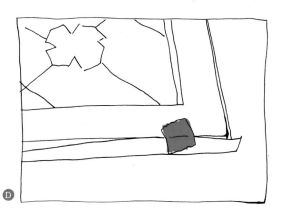

(D)

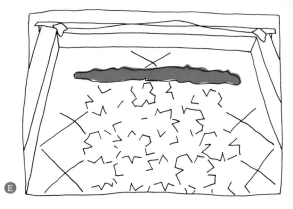

(E)

Ready to print

1. Take your T-shirt and slip a piece of newsprint inside – this will stop any ink from seeping through to the back. Tape it down flat onto a table and iron out any creases.

2. Lay one of your freshly cut stencils over the T-shirt where you want your print to be. Place the screen on top so that the mesh is touching the stencil and the cut-out area is in the middle. Make sure that the paper is bigger than the screen, so that there aren't any areas where the mesh touches the cotton (apart from in the areas you cut out). Now tape the stencil to the edge of the screen (fig D).

3. Spoon some yellow ink along the top edge of the screen, above the cut-out area, in a long, fat cucumber shape (fig E).

4. Almost ready to print! At this stage, it's a good idea to ask a friend to hold the screen down so that it doesn't slip about. Take the squeegee in two hands and hold at the very top of the screen. Tilt the squeegee towards you by about 45° (fig F), push down firmly and pull towards you, making sure you're pushing down all the time. Pull the ink over the screen, and stop just a little before the bottom edge.

5. Lift the squeegee up and put it back down on the other side of the ink. Using the same motion as before, push the ink back to the top of the screen. Once you've reached the top, lift the squeegee over the ink again and make one last pull as in step 4.

6. Scrape the ink off the squeegee and put it back in the pot. Hold the clean squeegee at the top of the screen and make one final pull as before, but without pulling any ink.

7. Put the squeegee down to one side and gently lift the screen off the print. Use a spoon to scrape off any excess ink from the screen. Peel the wet stencil off the screen and discard. In a sink or bath, wash the screen and squeegee in cold water. Leave the screen and the print to dry. This could take a couple of hours.

8. Lay another stencil over the first print, sliding it about a centimetre to the left so that it's slightly offset (fig G). Repeat steps 2-7 with blue ink.

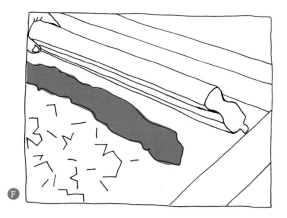

(F)

9. Place the last stencil over the print. This time align the stencil so that it is in between the first and second prints, and about 1cm lower (fig H). Repeat steps 2-7 using pink ink.

10. Once completely dry, cover the print with newsprint and iron for about three minutes. The heat will fix the ink to the cotton so that you can wash your shirt.

Sam Wingate lives and works in east London. From his Hackney studio he designs and produces a range of printed goods as clothing and for the home. His work is inspired by both urban life and also the practice of printing and drawing. *www.wingateprint.com, www.twitter.com/MrWingateLondon.*

Rain Blanken's
Fused Plastic Make-Up Bag

Yes, it is a plastic bag.
And it's never looked so chic.

Tools

~ dressmakers' pins
~ scissors
~ iron
~ sewing machine, or sewing
  needle

Materials

~ several plastic bags in various
  colours. Both thin and thicker
  plastic ones will work
~ clear plastic sandwich bag
~ approx 14cm zip
~ two sheets of A3 plain paper
~ small bits of tinsel or decorative
  plastic stuffing
~ sewing thread

What to do

Fusing plastic

1. Scout out the right bags for the job, bearing in mind colour and print.
2. Lay the plastic bag out flat and cut across the top to remove the handles. Then cut through both layers 1cm in from the sides and the bottom of the bag to create two flat pieces of plastic. Do this with two or three plastic bags.
3. Place a piece of blank paper on the ironing board, and neatly layer two or three pieces of plastic on top of one another, mixing colours – the most transparent or lighter colours work best on top. Finish off with another sheet of paper on top, making sure all the plastic is sandwiched in between paper (fig A) to avoid getting melted plastic on your ironing board and iron. You need to work in a well-ventilated area when fusing plastic with an iron, because the melted plastic has the potential to give off toxic fumes. An open-aired room or outdoor workspace is best.
4. Adjust the iron to the "rayon" setting. Pass the iron over the paper, moving it around a lot without pressing too hard, for 10 seconds. The constant movement of the heat will give a smooth finish, while pressing too hard in one spot will cause the plastic to bubble and deform. Peel up the paper to check your work. If some areas are not sticking together, concentrate on these for another 10 seconds (don't forget to put the paper back) until the plastic is nicely fused.

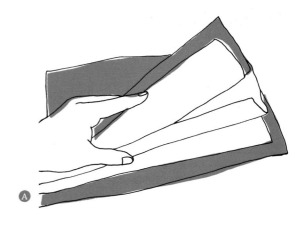

5. If you want to add more detail, cut out shapes (such as the pink and blue rectangles) from a contrasting plastic bag and arrange them on the already-fused plastic. For further embellishment, lay small strips of decorative plastic, such as tinsel strands, on top.
6. The sandwich bag is used to seal in the decorative pieces. Cut away the top and sides of the bag, then unfold it. Lay the bag on top of the arranged effects (fig B).
7. Iron again, with the paper on top and moving the iron the entire time, as before. The clear sandwich bag will melt over the effects.

> **TIP**
> The futuristic fused fabric can be used for any small-scale sewing projects.

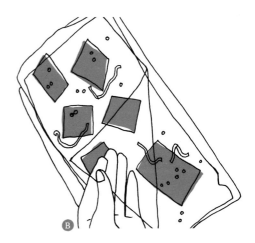

Making the bag

1. Fold the fused plastic sheet in half along the longest length, right sides together.
2. Sew up each side of the bag 1cm from the edge and stopping 2cm from the top. Use a straight stitch on a machine, or work a running stitch by hand.
3. At the top, fold over the 2cm allowance: fold one layer to one side and one to the other. Line the zip up on top of these folds, face down, with the teeth in the middle. Pin in place with the zip halfway open (fig C).
4. Stitch along each side of the zip 4mm-5mm away from the centre teeth (fig D). If you are using a machine, you can use the zip foot if you have one. If the zip is too long, snip off the bottom and run a zigzag stitch over the teeth at the end to create a new stopper.
5. Fold the zip flat at the top and sew up the sides of the purse again at the top to close any gaps between the side stitching and the zip, and to secure the zip to the bag.
6. Turn the purse right-side out. You have a new unique accessory – and you've saved the planet from a bit of plastic pollution.

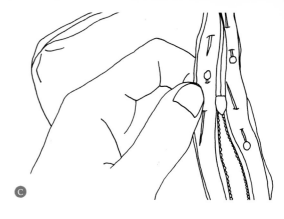

C

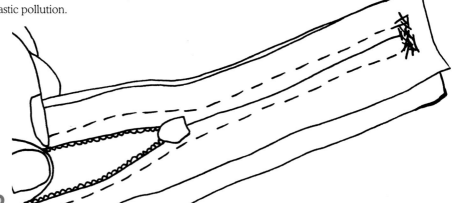

D

Rain Blanken is a full-time artist and writer, specialising in up-cycling, recycling and reinventing clothing. She tries out every kind of craft she can; still in search of the one she likes best. In the meantime, she is soaking up the exotic Ohio lifestyle with her family, building an army of tiny dogs, and most likely watching Conan O'Brien. *www.diyfashion.about.com, www.customizing-your-clothes.com.*

Tana West's **Anglepoise Jar Lamp**

A quirky jam-jar twist on a design classic – and a workout in woodwork construction.

Tools

~ 180-grade sandpaper, or similar
~ coping saw
~ junior hacksaw with a wood blade
~ hand or electric drill with 3mm and 6mm drill bits
~ clamp
~ ruler
~ set of compasses
~ tin snips
~ wood glue
~ cross-head screwdriver
~ flat-headed screwdriver
~ craft knife or wire stripper

Materials

~ old glass jar
~ approx 15cm x 25cm piece of 3mm plywood
~ 30cm x 20cm of 12mm-thick plywood
~ 38cm length of 2cm x 2cm square-section wood
~ four 6mm bolts with wing nuts (these come together in a pack)
~ lamp holder with E14 bulb (or similar) and shade holder (all available from electrical stores)
~ standard plug
~ 2m of 3-corded fabric-coated cable

What to do

1. Cut three lengths of the 2cm x 2cm wood, measuring 5cm, 15cm and 18cm. To do so, mark out the lengths in pencil, then clamp the wood to a surface you don't mind messing up a little (cover a section of a table with a protective piece of wood or, preferably, use a work bench) and cut with a junior hacksaw at a right angle.
2. Mark out the three strut templates twice on the 3mm plywood sheet (see templates on page 231), making sure measurements are exact. Clamp and cut out the straight, rectangular shapes using the coping saw. Keep moving and re-clamping the plywood as you go, and take your time – this requires a bit of patience, as the plywood is prone to splintering. Set the rectangular struts to one side.
3. Next, you need to work out the diameter of the jam jar opening. Measure across the top of the open jar, and add 2mm. Now redraw the jar holder template (also on page 231) on 3mm plywood, using this measurement as the diameter of the inner circle. Draw out the rest of the shape, ensuring that the space between the two slits is 2cm. Cut out the rectangle around this shape with the coping saw.
4. On the 12mm plywood, mark out four 15cm x 10cm rectangles and cut them out with the junior hacksaw. These will form the base. You now have all the elements roughly cut out.

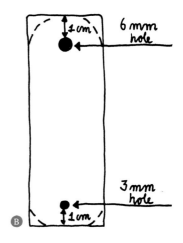

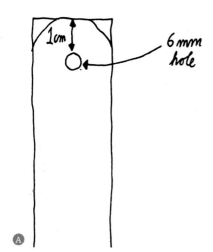

5. Now for drilling. First, use the 6mm drill bit. Take the 15cm and 18cm lengths of 2cm x 2cm wood, and drill holes at either end, right the way through, about 15mm from the end, and in the middle of the width. These are for the wing nuts.
6. Now make the corresponding holes in the plywood struts. Drill a hole, still with the 6mm bit, in either end of the two longest struts, 1cm in from the end, and in the centre of the width (fig A).
7. On two of the shorter struts (strut 2, which will go into the base), drill holes at one end only as in step 6.
8. On the other two short struts, drill, with the 6mm bit, a hole at one end, again 1cm from the end and in the middle of the width. Now switch to the 3mm bit, and drill holes at the other ends, again about 1cm from the end and in the middle of the width (fig B). This will join onto the part that holds the jar.

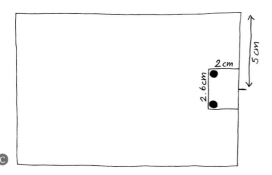

C

11. Now cut out the circle to hold the jar. With the coping saw, detach the blade at the end furthest away from the handle and thread the blade through one of the 6mm holes. Clamp the piece down and reattach the blade securely. Position the teeth against the line of the circle and start to gently saw around the circle. Re-clamp as you go to get a good position. Once the circle is fully cut out, detach the blade again to remove.

12. At the other end of this piece, you need to cut two short slits. Clamp again, and use the coping saw to saw two straight lines up to each of the 3mm drilled holes (fig E).

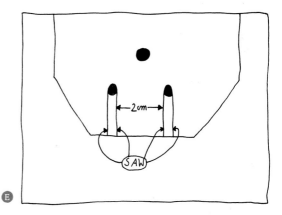

E

9. Now, on one of the 15cm x 10cm base pieces, mark out a rectangle measuring 2cm x 2.6cm at the centre of one 10cm side (fig C). In either inner corner of the rectangle, drill a hole with the 6mm bit.

10. More drilling! Now to tackle the section at the jar top. Drill holes as shown in fig D. For the four holes around the edge of the circle, use the 6mm bit. It doesn't matter where exactly they are around the circle, so long as they are close to the edge, as these are to help you cut out the circle. Now drill another 6mm hole in the centre of the section next to the circle. Switch to the 3mm bit, and drill the holes in the slit sections, about 1.5cm from the edge. These are to form the slits that will slot onto the top strut. As mentioned before, it is very important that the slits are 2cm apart, so double-check your measurements before you drill.

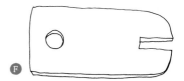

F

13. On the struts with the 3mm holes at one end, make the slits as in step 12 (fig F).

14. Now for the top base part, the one with the holes drilled in it. Saw along the straight lines of the 2cm x 2.6cm rectangle, using the drilled holes to help you round the corners.

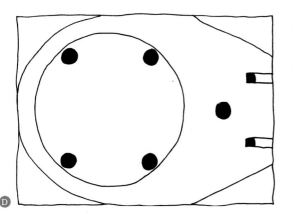

D

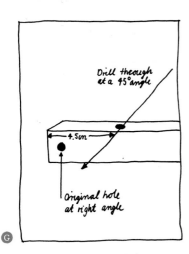

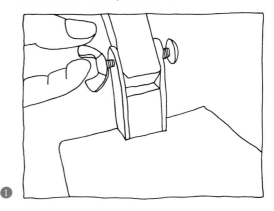

19. Now for the jar. Remove the lid and draw a circle in the centre the same size as the top section of the lampshade holder (the bit that sticks up). Drill a few holes around the inner edge of this circle, and use the tin snips to carefully cut it out (it is quite sharp when cut, so watch your hands).

15. Now to drill the wire holes in the two longer lengths of 2cm x 2cm wood. On the sides that have no holes drilled into them, drill a hole about 4.5cm from either end. Use the 6mm drill bit and drill at a 45° angle, pointing the drill toward the end of the wood (fig G).

16. And so to sanding. Following the templates, round the corners of the struts that have curves using sandpaper up to your marked-out lines. Then gently sand all the cut edges till smooth.

17. Now for gluing. Glue the four base rectangles together with plenty of wood glue, making sure the one with the small rectangle cut out of it is on the top. Clamp and leave to dry. It usually takes about an hour.

18. Glue the two short struts with just one hole at one end (strut 2) to the 5cm length of 2cm x 2cm wood. Lining up the straight edges, so that the curved ends of the plywood stick out of the top, and glue it straight into the space in the base (fig H). If it doesn't fit exactly, sand it down till it does. Leave to dry.

20. Once the base is fully dry, you can attach all the struts with the bolts and wing nuts. Start with the 18cm length of 2cm x 2cm wood, positioning it between the plywood connected to the base so that the 45° holes 4.5cm from the end are on the outside edge. Simply push the bolt through the plywood, then the wood and second plywood section, and screw on the wing nut (fig I). Screw it tight enough that the struts will stand up, but so that you can still move it – you might need a screwdriver to hold the screw side still.

21. In the same way add the remaining struts in this order: long plywood struts; 15cm piece of 2cm x 2cm wood (again, the 45° holes at 4.5cm should be on the outside edge); short struts with slits.

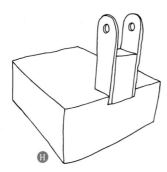

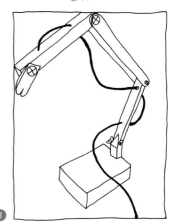

K

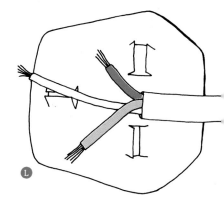

L

22. Thread the electrical cable through the angled holes, starting at the bottom hole on the side (fig J). Pull the cable through so that you so have about 15cm spare after the last hole.

23. Now you want to wire up the lamp holder, which may or may not come with instructions. At the end of each cable, use a craft knife to carefully score around the fabric covering 3cm from the end and remove, making sure the internal wires are intact. Then strip the fabric cover carefully off the separate wires 6mm from the ends. Twist the exposed copper wires together on each strip. (If you are not confident doing this, ask someone to help, or look it up online.)

24. Thread the jar lid onto the end of the wire, then wire up the electrical connections in the lamp holder. The live wire is brown, blue is neutral, and the green and yellow wire is the earth. The live and neutral wires go into the matching contacts, while earth goes in the separate connector (fig K). If in any doubt, please check with someone that you have it wired correctly. Using a flat-headed screwdriver, unscrew the electrical contacts enough to push the wires into place, then screw tight again and pull to check they are secure. Fit the lamp holder together.

25. At the other end of the cable, you want to fit the plug. Open up the plug with a screwdriver and strip the cable as before. Strip the individual cables to 6mm of bare copper wire, and twist. Wire the plug as shown on the diagram supplied with it (fig L). Make sure you have wired it correctly and all connections are secure before closing the plug. Add a bulb and check it all works.

26. Now screw the jar body into the jar holder piece of plywood, and then slot the holder on the struts. Then simply screw the jar together (fig M).

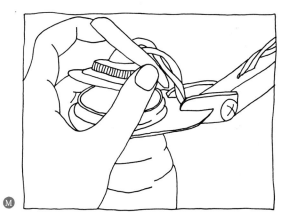

M

Tana West is an artist living and working in east London. After studying sculpture at Central Saint Martins College of Art and Design, and making many moths from tumble-dryer fluff, she continues to use a mixture of found and fabricated items to create things that are both functional and non-functional, from objects to installations. Tana's design repertoire is eclectic; although working predominantly in ceramics, she makes resourceful use of whatever materials are to hand. *www.tanawest.co.uk.*

Interview with Erin Dollar

What are your earliest crafting memories? I fondly remember dyeing Easter eggs in the traditional Ukrainian method, using a delicate wax resist and many layers of dye. I really loved working on intricate projects and designs, and found an appreciation for the handmade very early on in life. I think labouring over those eggs as a kid really reinforced the idea that there is value in handmade things, and that the love and care that goes into making a work of art is obvious to those who encounter it.

You recently shut down your beard shop - how come? To be quite honest, the beard project was simply taking up too much of my time. As an artist, I like to take on a variety of projects, and making beards full time was keeping me from pursuing other artistic endeavours I was interested in. While I absolutely loved creating each beard, and my customers and fans were seriously some of the coolest people I've met, I felt that the beard project had run its course after three years, and that it was a good time to move on to other, non-hairy, projects.

What craft projects are you up to now? Right now I am throwing myself, full force, into printmaking, which is my biggest passion. I am creating lots of new works on paper, as well as developing a line of limited-edition and one-of-a-kind home goods. I'm exploring patterns and fabrics, which is so much fun, and keeps me close to my well-loved sewing machine.

How did I Made You a Beard come about? My beard project came about completely by accident. I made my first beard during my finals week at college, as a side project to distract myself from looming deadlines. The first beard was hilarious, very shaggy and unkempt, and it brought a smile to my friends' faces as we studied for exams. The beard was at that point a very big part of hipster culture and so it seemed a fun, tongue-in-cheek, playful way to examine masculinity. For months after that, my friends were requesting that I make them their own beards, and it got to be so popular that I opened an Etsy shop on a whim. The shop became very busy and as I perfected my beard-making techniques, I decided to become a full-time beard-maker. I figured, "Why not?"

Where do you get your craft inspiration? I try not to take myself too seriously and to just focus on making things that make me happy. Sure, I will certainly spend three weeks labouring over a fine art relief print, spending hours trying to get everything perfect, but I'll also take time to just draw a silly portrait of my cat once in a while. I think it's really important not to always worry about building a cohesive portfolio, and to just enjoy the process of making things. I am endlessly inspired by my artist friends; it's wonderfully motivating to be surrounded by creative people.

Do you look at any specific websites for inspiration or practical tips? I love the Purl Bee blog; they have so many wonderful sewing tutorials. Whipup has also been an extremely useful resource for me; I think you can find tutorials for just about anything on there. In general, I think Becky Johnson of Sweetie Pie Press and Faythe Levine of Handmade Nation have been my guides to the world of handmade, and I look to their blogs for inspiration and guidance. [www.purlbee.com, whipup. net, www.sweetiepiepress.com, handmadenationmovie.com.]

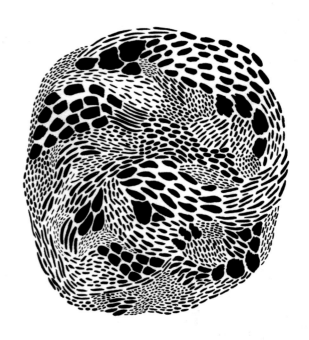

What's the best thing you've ever made? That's a tough question! I think the thing I'm most proud of is a 12-colour woodcut print of an imaginary landscape, which measures 56cm x 76cm, and is the largest, most detailed print I've ever attempted. Although, I think maybe the best thing I've ever made is a 60cm-long replica of my friend Jack Passion's beard - his beard is recognised as one of the best in the world!

What's the worst thing you've ever made? I've had lots of inedible botched baking experiments, which I think would certainly qualify as some of the worst things I've ever made. Art-wise, I've drawn a lot of really bad sketches and unsalvageable paintings. For me, making art is often trial and error, and while I certainly look back on much of my old work and grimace, I think that's just part of the process of growing as an artist.

Where do you craft? Mostly at home, in Pasadena, California: I am lucky enough to have a boyfriend who doesn't mind that I've taken over most of the house with my art supplies and half-finished projects. I've built a small studio space in my living room, complete with a sewing table, plus a large table that holds my printing press and all my printing supplies.

What is your dream craft project? I mostly dream about collaborating with artists I love and respect, such as Yayoi Kusama, Camilla Engman or Keri Smith. Getting an opportunity to work with famous artists, or just a large group of talented artist friends, is something I'm always trying to pursue.

Do you feel part of a craft scene or movement? I'd like to think that I'm a small cog in the machine of the handmade movement! After participating in many shows and craft fairs, I feel very connected to the craft community here on the West Coast, and I feel lucky to have met so many talented people along the way.

Erin Dollar's
Mysterious Moustache Disguise

Need a quick disguise?
Go incognito with some
homemade facial hair.

Tools
~ dressmakers' pins
~ scissors
~ sewing machine, or
  sewing needle

Materials
~ 20cm x 30cm piece of felt,
  any colour
~ thread in matching colour
~ 60cm of clear elastic cord, such
  as Stretch Magic (found in the
  beading or jewellery section of
  craft stores)
~ paper

What to do

1. Copy the moustache template on page 230 onto a piece of paper – or make your own design – and cut out. Hold the template up to your face: if you want to tweak the shape, now is the time to do so.
2. Fold the piece of felt in half and pin the template to both layers. Cut around the template to create two matching moustache pieces. Remove the template and pins.
3. Measure (using string or the clear elastic) around the circumference of your head, starting at the centre of your mouth, circling back over the ears and behind the head, where the strap will rest. Cut a piece of the clear elastic to this length (probably around 50cm-56cm) and tie a large knot (made up of five or six individual knots) as close to each end as possible.
4. Position the two knots at either end of one felt moustache (fig A). Place the second moustache on top, sandwiching the elastic between the felt layers so the knots are hidden. Pin in place, making sure to secure the elastic symmetrically on each side of the moustache, so it will lay flat on your face.
5. Sew around the moustache 3mm from the fabric edge with a straight running stitch (fig B). Sew an extra couple of stitches over the elastic to make sure it's held firmly in place. Trim stray threads and messy edges, and try on the moustache.

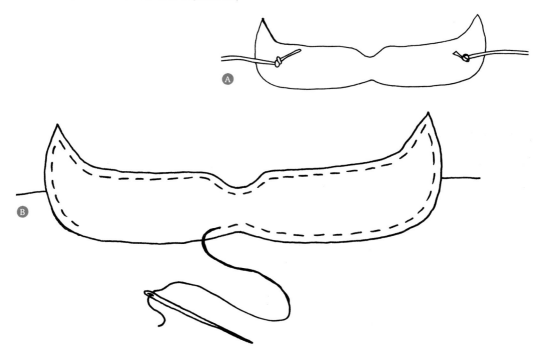

Erin Dollar is an artist and maker of awesome things living in Los Angeles. She is the beard-maker behind I Made You a Beard and her beards have been warming the faces of the earth since 2007. When she's not sewing or printing, you can find her riding her bike or writing letters to her many pen pals. *www.imadeyouabeard.com*.

Lucky Bird's **Recycled Planters**

By Kim Jenkins

Breathing new life into market leftovers.

....

Tools
~ scissors
~ sewing machine

....

Materials
~ old vegetable sack or anything strong enough to stand on its own: strong plastic, builders sacks etc
~ approx 20cm of string/ cord
~ 3cm thick polypropolene webbing the same length as the width of the sack

What to do

1. Give the sack a good wipe – they can be quite smelly – then cut it in half. If you have a sack with an image band across the middle, cut about 4cm above the image and about 10cm below it (fig A). Otherwise, you want the piece to be approx 30cm high and 45cm across.

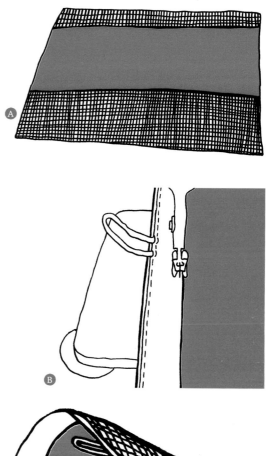

3. Cut a piece of webbing to fit along the width of the sacking you just cut out.
4. Fold the 4cm top bit of net over to the wrong side of the sack and place the webbing on top of the fold on the right side. Sew three-quarters of the way along the top of the webbing. Keep the sack under the sewing machine foot and make the cord into a loop. Tuck the ends of the loop between the webbing and the sack (fig B), then continue to sew, trapping the cord.
5. Sew along the other edge of the webbing.
6. Fold the piece in half so that the two edges of the webbing join up and the right sides are facing. Sew along the side, about 1cm in from the edge.
7. At the bottom, fold over the edge twice to one side, hiding the rough edge; sew the fold into place just under the image band or about 22cm down from the top edge. You will now have a pocket.
8. Now you want to give the pocket a square base. This is a little tricky. Stand the planter up, lining up the seam on the side to the seam at the bottom. The corner will stick out to the side, making a triangle (fig C). Fold up the triangle: this fold should be at a right angle to the side seam. Sew along the crease at the bottom of the triangle.
9. Repeat step 8 on the other side, although here you will need to match the side fold with the bottom seam. Make sure the triangles are the same size on both side, otherwise you'll have a wonky bottom!
10. Turn the planter right-side out.

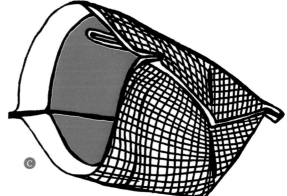

Kim Jenkins teaches printmaking alongside creating her own printed products, which she sells at London's Broadway Market – also an ideal place to find valuable source materials. Several market traders save their vegetable sacks for her, but she can still be found trawling through rubbish at the end of the day. Kim is into cycling as well as recycling, heading off on biking holidays whenever she can. *www.luckybird.co.uk.*

I CAN Make Shoes' **Summer Sandals**

by Amanda Luisa

If the idea of making your own shoes seems a step too far, think again…

Tools

~ scissors
~ masking tape
~ brush or spatula
~ a helping pair of hands is useful!

Materials

(available from I CAN Make Shoes and general haberdashery shops)

~ pair of insole boards
~ pair of foam inserts
~ pair of soles
~ tub of Neoprene glue
~ approx 40cm x 40cm piece of material to cover insoles – you can use anything you have lying around the house; this example uses an old pair of pyjamas
~ approx 320cm of rope or ribbon etc for straps (this pair uses 70cm of 2.5cm-wide suede trim or grosgrain ribbon and 250cm of rope cord)

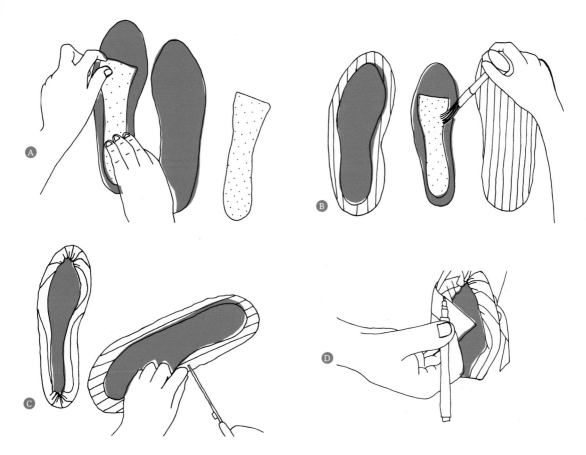

What to do

1. Position the insole boards in front of you, with the right and left on the correct sides. Glue the foam inserts onto the insole boards at the centre back (fig A). Apply a small amount of glue to both parts that you will be joining, then leave the glue to go tacky (and almost dry) before you press the two pieces together.

2. Place the insoles onto the wrong side of the material, and draw around the shapes 1cm from the edge. Cut out along these lines.

3. Brush a small amount of glue onto the whole top surfaces of the insoles (the side with the foam stuck to it); then apply a small amount of glue to the wrong side of the pieces of material. Again, wait until the glue is almost completely dry before you press the insoles into the middle of the material (fig B). Smooth over the fabric with your fingertips, making sure there are no air bubbles between the foam and the insole.

4. Apply a small amount of glue around the edges of the insole. Fold the excess material over and stick it to the sole – you'll need to fold the fabric over itself at the toe and the heel and snip into it to stretch it round the sides (fig C). Take your time to make sure the fabric is stretched neatly all around the insole.

5. You may need a friend to help you at this stage. In this case, the toes will be crossed with two straps. For each sandal, cut about 25cm of the suede trim and position at the front of the insole at a slight diagonal. With your foot inside, tape the straps in position underneath the insole and mark on them where you want them to fold underneath, so that they fit you snugly (fig D).

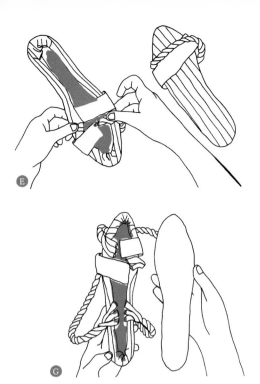

E

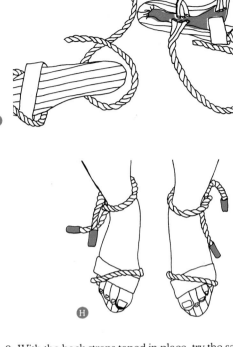

F

G

H

6. Repeat step 5 with a 25cm length of rope for each sandal, crossing over the suede in the opposite diagonal direction (fig E).

7. The back straps (two on each sandal) will wrap around the ankle. Cut two pieces of rope measuring approx 40cm and another two measuring 50cm. The shorter pieces go on the inside of the foot, and the longer ones on the outside; tape them to the insole along the side from the heel (fig F). When positioning the back straps it is important that they are pointing slightly backwards towards the heel so that they wrap neatly around the ankle.

8. With the back straps taped in place, try the sandal on, gently tying up the ankle straps. Adjust until they feel snug. Mark out clearly where the straps should fold onto the insole. Glue all the straps in place, again applying glue to both the insole and the strap, waiting for it to go tacky, then pressing firmly together.

9. Trim any loose pieces of material, rope etc to minimise bulk. Apply an even amount of glue to both the entire bottom of the insoles and the top of the sole (the side without the grip); once they have nearly completely dried, stick the two together (fig G).

10. To finish, cut four short strips (approx 6cm-7cm) of the suede trim, glue and wrap around the rope ends (fig H). Finished! Now you can tell the world, "I CAN make shoes!"

Amanda Luisa set up I CAN Make Shoes in early 2010. After many successful years as a shoemaker, Amanda developed a modern method of shoe-making that gave her the freedom to start doing it from home. The high demand for these skills prompted her to develop a variety of London-based shoe-making workshops, which have already helped to launch the careers of some very exciting new shoe designers. *www.icanmakeshoes.com.*

Crafthouse's **Fabric Coasters**

By Kate Alsanjak

Make coasters to match your living room – or in colours to match your mood, and your mugs.

Tools

~ dressmakers' pins
~ sewing needle
~ knitting needle, or other pointed implement
~ scissors
~ iron
~ tailors' chalk, or a pencil
~ sewing machine (optional)

Materials

~ enough fabric per coaster to make two squares measuring 11cm x 11cm – a medium-weight cotton or linen works best
~ medium-weight iron-on interfacing measuring 11cm x 11cm per coaster
~ sewing thread
~ ribbons, embroidery thread etc for your design

What to do

1. Make a square paper template for the coasters measuring 11cm x 11cm. This includes a 1cm seam allowance (fig A).
2. Using the template, draw two squares on the fabric and one square on the interfacing for each coaster. Cut out along the lines.
3. On the wrong side of the fabric, iron the interfacing onto one of the fabric squares; this will be the back of your coasters.
4. For the top side of the coasters, the design options are endless, and can be made by hand stitching or using a sewing machine. Here are some examples:
   a. Tie a bow with lightweight wide ribbon and pin it onto your fabric. Iron the bow as flat as possible; then sew around the edges (fig B).

TIP

The same technique can be used to make tablemats, using pieces of fabric and facing measuring approx 25cm x 35cm.

   b. Criss-cross wool or embroidery threads across the square in random designs. Tape the threads down at the edges to hold in place, then sew evenly spaced lines every 1cm or so across the fabric to secure. You can use a mix of straight stitching and zigzig stitches on a machine.
   c. Use stripes or gingham checked fabrics as the base and add threads as above, following the lines of the pattern to create a more graphic design. Stitch over the threads with a zigzag stitch.

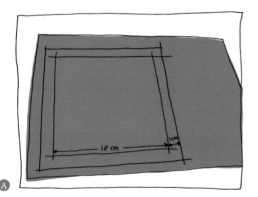

A

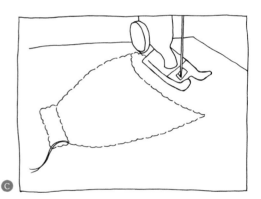

C

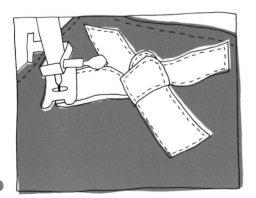

B

   d. Draw out a more detailed design, such as the teacup, on paper; then stick the paper design onto the window, place a fabric square on top and trace the pattern onto the fabric in chalk or pencil. Stitch the design with your sewing machine or by hand (fig C).
5. Now place the two halves of the coaster right sides together and stitch around all four edges, leaving a 3cm opening in one corner.

6. While the coaster is still inside out, trim the fabric diagonally across the three stitched corners, taking care not to cut into the stitches (fig D) – this will reduce bulk and give a crisper finish.

7. Turn the fabric right side out, pushing the fabric through the opening with a knitting needle. Push the knitting needle right into the corners to give a sharp square edge.

8. Iron the coaster flat, turning the rough edges in at the open corner. Sew up the gap by hand with a whipstitch. You can also stitch a border around the edge.

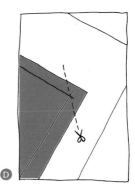

Kate Alsanjak lives in Hastings, on the south coast of England, with her husband and too many rolls of fabric. Kate has been sewing and crafting since she could hold a needle and also loves to bake. 2011 sees the launch of Bake and Crafthouse, a new concept offering craft and cooking classes for kids. *www.bakeandcrafthouse.com*.

Interview with Prick Your Finger's Rachael Matthews and Louise Harries

Louise Harries, left, and Rachael Matthews in front of their east London shop

How did you get into craft?

R: I can't really remember. My mother would try me on all different crafts, then I got my first sewing machine when I was about six, and that was the thing.

L: I just always wanted to make things. I would driving everyone mad going, "I want to make something." I was always fiddling with something. I used to do a lot of paper craft, like quilling. And then my aunty taught me to knit, when I was about seven or eight. Just squares that I used to sew up into doll's clothes.

R: I think I started making things because I was frustrated that I couldn't buy them. You'd see stuff on the telly – on *Top of the Pops* maybe – but there weren't any shops in the Lake District to buy that kind of stuff, and I didn't have enough pocket money anyway. That's the thing isn't it: you want things. I had to learn to take my trousers in to get them tight because my mum would never buy me that stuff. Also, when I was at boarding school, I used to make clothes and pretend that I had bought them. But then it's to never stop doing it. That's when you know you're crafty, when you can't stop.

When did you think you could do craft as a career?

R: When I wasn't allowed to do it at school. We didn't do art at school. I was absolutely furious, because I realised that it was all I wanted to do.

L: I studied textiles at Saint Martins [College of Art and Design], which was very machine-based and any time you did something with your hands they thought you were a bit odd. I remember being told I'd never get a job with knitting if I didn't machine knit. But all the jobs I've ever done in fashion are because I can hand-knit.

What is the greatest thing you've ever made?

L: I haven't made it yet! I'll let you know when I have. I forget about everything I've made.

R: It's really hard to say because when I've finished making something I sort of lose interest. I'm so delighted that I've finished it and I can move onto the next thing, that I don't really even like looking at what I've made. Every piece I'm making, I think, "This is going to be the thing." And then it's like, "Finished. Next!"

What is your ultimate dream craft project?

L: A light-up cloak – that's what I'm working on. It might flash messages.

R: There are too many that I want to do. I've just made this explosion jumper, and that was a bit of an undertaking, so I just want to do simple things this year.

How long did the explosion jumper take?

R: The conception took a nano-second. I just thought, "I want to knit an explosion." I didn't know it was going to be a jumper, but I just started. Because it sort of had to go everywhere, I could pick up bits of it at different times, but it took me a year to do it. Normally, I would go back to knitting it because something explosive had happened, or I felt explosive. It was a nice thing to live with but it blew my life apart trying to get the bloody thing together.

Projects can ruin you life. Every project has a bit of a pain barrier. I love that. If you conquer the pain barrier, it's brilliant. The worst thing is leaving a half-finished project; that is really horrible. You think, "Oh, I'll come back to that later," but you won't keep the momentum going with it.

I did this thing called the UFO [Unfinished Object] Administration Service for the Jerwood Prize a couple of years ago, where people sent in their unfinished objects with a story attached. We gave the projects out to different people to finish them off with the story in mind. It's really hard to take something on when it's somebody else's problem, but everyone that took on a UFO completed it. They all struggled, but everyone had quite a profound experience.

What people inspire you?

L: People who are slightly visionary, who go against the grain and do things even though people think they are a bit odd.

R: My projects are always made for someone or made for a situation, and it's the things going on around me that inspire it, rather than looking at other artists' work.

Where do you craft?

R: My favourite place to make things is in the passenger seat of a car, in daylight on a long motorway. It has to be a car with a nice big dashboard so I can lay everything out. Trains are too squashed; it doesn't work so well. I can get so much done in a car.

L: I can never do that. I don't have a particular place. Wherever. It depends what it is. Quite often it's my kitchen.

R: I do like an intense knitting project; at a desk with a bright light, and a lot of thinking.

What is the state of craft at the moment?

R: Well, a few years ago, I was always going on telly or being in the papers, and we had to keep doing it to keep the craft scene going. But it doesn't need that any more. Before, everybody was writing about it like it was this hot new thing. And in a way it was, because we were out in public spaces and that was new, but the actual people that came together had always been knitting, pretty much. It's not really "back"; it never goes away. It's in your DNA. There's definitely a really hardcore scene of people that have always got several projects on the go. But it's not a clique; it's all different scenes of people, and all ages.

About five or six years ago, I would go and teach kids to knit and they would all bring out the granny jokes, but if I teach kids now they think it's completely normal. There's no, "Oh, my gran used to knit." It has become more mainstream, which is really good. It's not going away.

*Rachael Matthews'
explosion jumper*

Rachael Matthews' **Between a Rock and a Hard Place Cardigan**

Work a woolly story into an old, unloved cardigan with a frenzy of French knitting.

Tools
~ dressmakers' pins
~ French knitting dolly
~ large knitter's bodkin needle
~ cardboard for making pom-poms, or a pom-pom maker

Materials
~ an old cardigan or jumper
~ lots of odds and ends of wool yarn

Skills
~ French knitting
~ pom-poms

"Walking home one day, I sighted upon a duck-egg blue lambswool cardigan lying in a puddle in the road. Always partial to duck-egg blue, I stared at it for a while. Filthy, dirty, discarded, left to rot in the gutter, it spoke out to me, asking me to question why a perfectly sound fabric should appear dangerous and wrong to touch. Picking it up, I took it home to the safety of a 60° cycle in the washing machine. Slightly felted, out of shape and missing some buttons, this cardigan was to be reborn…"

What to do

1. Pick out half-used balls of wool and arrange a colour palette to suit your cardigan or jumper. Then make as much French knitting and as many pom-poms (pages 26 and 28 respectively) as you can. This cardigan, which is decorated on the back as well as the front, uses over 10m of French knitting, which takes hours and hours – so get going! You can always make more pom-poms and French knitting once you have started to attach them to the cardigan.

2. Take a section of the French-knit tube and start to arrange it on the cardigan. Think about the grain in wood, lines in rock, or patterns left behind by the sea on the beach. Pin in place as you go.

3. Once happy with the position, thread a length of the same yarn through the yarn needle, and using a loose backstitch, start sewing on the French-knit embellishments, going through the tubes into the inside of the cardigan and back out (fig A).

4. You will begin to form spaces where pom-poms can nest and different colours of French knitting can work together. Just sew the pom-poms on with the tail from around the middle, securing with a few stitches in the same spot on the cardigan.

5. The more you work, the more elaborate it will become. As it thickens, it develops more shape, weight, and power. The only problem you'll have is knowing when to call it finished…

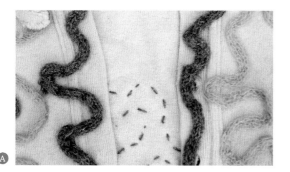

A

"Half finished, this cardigan was worn to parties with the needle on the lapel and a ball of French knitting in the pocket. It became a great talking point as I worked."

Rachael Matthews was born in the Lake District with frizzy hair, nimble fingers and a romantic disposition, which has led her to dedicate her life to the promotion of hand knitting as a tool for change and to reignite the British wool industry with the help of her trusty friend Louise. They now run a wool shop/museum called Prick Your Finger in London. Her favourite hobbies are drawing, writing postcards, messing around in boats and foraging. *www.prickyourfinger.com.*

Louise Harries' **Crochet Collar**

Top off an old T-shirt with, well, an old T-shirt – or rather, one that's been hooked up into a natty detachable collar.

Tools

~ 8mm crochet hook

Materials

~ cone of Hoopla yarn (an upcycled jersey yarn), or a couple of old T-shirts to chop up

Skills

~ chain
~ slip stitch
~ double crochet
~ treble crochet

What to do

1. If you are making your own yarn from a T-shirt, cut along the seams to separate the back and the body, then starting at the bottom, cut a 1cm-thick strip across. Stop 1cm from the edge, turn and cut the other way. Repeat up the fabric.
2. With the 8mm crochet hook, 42ch.
3. You are going to work on the collar one half at a time, leaving half of the base chain to work on later. Work the first half as follows:
   Row 1: 1dc into each of the first 20 chain spaces (20 dc).
   Row 2: first, make two turning chains. Then *sk1, 1tr; rep from * to end of row (11tr worked, including the turning chain).
4. To work the second half, miss one chain space along from the first half, then repeat rows 1-2 as before.
5. Now for the loops around the outside edge of the collar. Starting at the top right-hand corner, attach the yarn with a slip stitch then 7ch. Fasten down with a slip stitch at the bottom corner to make the first loop. Make another 7ch, sk2 and fasten with a slip stitch to make a second loop. Carry on along the edge of the collar so that each half has one loop at the edge and six along the bottom.

Lousie Harries used to work in fashion and is now one half of Prick Your Finger, the rock n' roll haberdashery in Bethnal Green, east London. Besides doing a LOT of knitting, crocheting and sewing, and more recently macrame, she likes to dress up as Axel Rose and play the banjo, especially when doing the shop's accounts. She has a secret crush on William Morris, collects Cazel glasses and is quite good at painting bad portraits. *www.prickyourfinger.com.*

By Elizabeth Hawkridge

A stash for your cash, nautical style.

Tools

~ dressmakers' pins
~ sewing needle
~ scissors
~ ruler
~ tailors' chalk, or pencil
~ sewing machine (optional)

Materials

For Mr Sailor Whale feltie

~ approx 10cm x 10cm pieces of felt in dark blue, white and sea blue
~ 10cm x 10cm piece of thicker white felt
~ white cat's-eye button
~ silver anchor shank button
~ approx 18 pearly white seed beads
~ embroidery thread in black and light blue
~ sewing thread in black and white
~ small piece of iron-on webbing or all-purpose glue
~ 40cm of approx 2.5cm-wide iron-on hemming (optional)

For the purse

~ navy blue 15cm zip (a larger zip can be cut down)
~ iron-on hemming (optional)
~ 20cm x 40cm of lining fabric
~ 20cm x 40cm striped fabric

For extra zip decoration

~ two strands of ribbon approx 30cm long
~ two jump rings
~ a little charm, such as an anchor
~ miniature lobster swivel clip

What to do

Mr Sailor Whale feltie

1. Cut out the felt pieces using the template on page 232: whale body and fin in blue; belly in white and sea blue for the water spurt.
2. Use small pieces of iron-on webbing or a few dabs of glue to join the fin and belly to the whale body; then attach this piece and the water spurt to the square of thick white felt. Cut around the whale leaving a 5mm-wide border (fig A).
3. With the tailors' chalk, draw four lines on the whale's belly. Sew along these lines in black thread, using a backstitch.
4. Cut a length of the black embroidery thread and divide the strands in half, so you are working with just three strands. Using a running stitch, sew around the whale, the fin and belly (fig B).
5. Do the same with the blue embroidery thread; then stitch around the water spurt with a backstitch.

6. Make a small slit on the whale's body just below the tail; pop the shank (the loop at the back) of the silver anchor button into this hole, and sew into place on the back of the whale. Then sew on the white button for the whale's eye.

7. To finish, sew on the white pearly beads (fig C).

C

The purse

1. Cut four pieces of fabric measuring roughly 18cm x 18cm: two for the outer layer, and two for the lining. It helps to make the fabric the same length as the zip you are using.

2. Position the whale feltie centrally on one piece of outer fabric and attach with a running stitch through the white border.

3. On all four pieces of fabric, fold over 1cm-2cm along the top edge, so that the wrong sides of the fabric are touching. Iron to hold the folds in place. If you have iron-on hemming, iron this on over the folds.

4. Take the piece of outer fabric with the whale on it and place it face down. Put the zip on top of the folded edge face down (so that the zip teeth cannot be seen). Then place the folded edge of a lining piece face up (so you can't see the rough edge of the fold) onto the zip (fig D). Pin in place, making sure the zip and fabrics are aligned. You end up with a fabric and zip sandwich, with 1mm-2mm of the zip braid and the teeth poking out of the top.

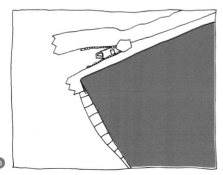

D

5. With the outer fabric facing up towards you, sew a straight stitch line (or a running stitch if you are working by hand) along the top of the fabric next to the zip (fig E). Pull the zip slightly open when sewing as this allows for tautness.

6. Repeating steps 4 and 5, attach the remaining fabric to the other side of the zip. Make a sandwich in exactly the same way with the other half of the zip.

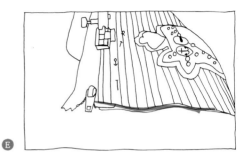

E

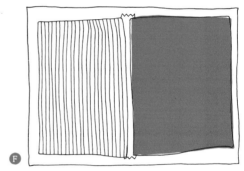

F

7. Now it is now time to sew up the purse. Before you begin, pull the zip open halfway and leave it there – this comes in handy later! Pull both the lining parts to one side of the zip, and the two outer parts to the other side, so that the right sides of the fabric are facing together (fig F). Pin the two layers together on both sides.

8. Starting at one bottom corner of the lining, sew 1cm in from the edge to the opposite bottom corner of the outer fabric, going over the zip. Continue to sew round the perimeter of the rectangle, but stop 5cm from the starting point to create a turning gap in the bottom of the lining (fig G).

9. Cut the four corners of the fabric diagonally, being careful not to snip any stitching, and cut the ends of the zip so that only 3mm-4mm sticks out beyond the stitching. This de-bulking gives a neater finish.

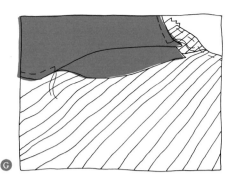

10. Turn the whole thing the right way out through that turning gap in the bottom of the lining. I warn you, it will look messy (fig H); but keep going, and you will discover why you left the zip half open earlier…

11. Now pull the lining out to sew up the gap at the bottom. Fold in the rough edges and press flat. Sew along the edge to close.

12. Before popping the lining back in, iron it a little; iron the outside too while you're at it. Neat!

13. For the zip decoration, tie both of the strands of ribbon in the centre to a jump ring. Add the charm to one jump ring. Attach the rings to a miniature lobster swivel clip; then clip this to the zip pull.

"You can follow the purse section of these instructions to make a plain pouch; or just sew a Mr Sailor Whale and wear him as a brooch."

Elizabeth Hawkridge lives in Pembrokeshire, Wales, in a small town called Milford Haven, where she is a designer-maker and creater of unique handmade felt brooches and accessories. She gets lots of inspiration from nature, animals and her surrounding environment. Lizzybeth's Felties emerged from her long-time love of being creative and her favourite tactile elements such as buttons, ribbons and beads. *lizzybeths-felties.blogspot.com, www.folksy.com/shops/lizzybethsfelties.*

Kirsty Neale's **Paper Fruits**

Fashion paper into fun faux-fruit decorations.

Tools

~ scissors
~ ruler

Materials

~ piece of cardboard, such as a cereal box
~ several sheets of patterned paper, such as wrapping or art paper (wood grain looks especially dramatic), glossy magazines, old maps, the insides of security envelopes, pages from an old book etc
~ A4 sheet of brown paper
~ glue stick
~ PVA glue
~ scrap of green felt

What to do

1. Draw out an apple or pear shape about 7.5cm high or 12cm high respectively. Copy it onto the card and cut out.

2. Draw around the fruit template onto the back of your chosen patterned paper. Cut the paper shape out and repeat, making a total of 30-50 pieces, depending on the thickness of the paper you are using. You can always cut more later. If your paper is fairly thin, try cutting through several layers at once to save time.

3. Fold each paper shape in half lengthways. Press the folds down firmly to create a nice, sharp crease.

4. Take two shapes. On the back of one, cover the area left of the centre fold with glue from the glue stick. Press the right-hand section of the second shape down on top of it, so your two pieces are half glued together, half free (fig A).

5. Now apply glue to the left-hand side of the second apple. Press the right-hand section of a third shape down on top of it. Keep repeating this action, sticking the paper shapes together half-back to half-back. The fruit should quite quickly start to form a round shape when you stand it up.

6. Once you've used up all the paper shapes and are happy with how the fruit looks, spread glue over the left-hand side of the final piece and press it against the right-hand side of the first one to join both ends of the apple or pear together.

7. Cut a piece of brown paper measuring approx 15cm x 15cm for the pear, or a 10cm x 15cm piece for the apple, and roll it into a cigar shape. Make the roll as tight as you can and check it fits snugly into the hole that runs through the centre of the fruit. (You might need to adjust the size of the brown paper rectangle, depending on the type of paper you've used to construct the fruit. Thicker sheets will tend to make a larger "core" at the centre. Experiment with a piece of scrap paper first.)

8. Once you've made any adjustments, unwrap the roll, spread some PVA glue over the paper and re-wrap.

9. Cut a leaf shape with a narrow stalk from green felt.

10. Spread more PVA glue over the outside of your paper stalk and push it down into the centre of your fruit, then press the leaf to the top of the stalk. Leave to dry thoroughly.

11. Fan out the paper pieces, adjusting so they're evenly spaced.

> **TIP**
> This technique will work with just about any symmetrical shape. If it doesn't have a flat base, you can always add a length of ribbon and create a hanging decoration.

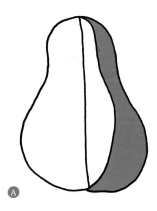

A

Kirsty Neale works as a freelance writer and designer, and has always loved to make things. When she was five, one of her drawings was shown in the gallery on children's TV programme *Take Hart*. It won her a prize – a smart, hardback book – and she feels very lucky that, 30 years on, she's still able to fund her book habit by making things and sharing them with people. *kirstyneale.typepad.com, www.etsy.com/shop/helloclementine*.

Sugar Paper's **Needle Book Classic**

By Seleena Laverne Daye

Give your sewing needles a home of their own.

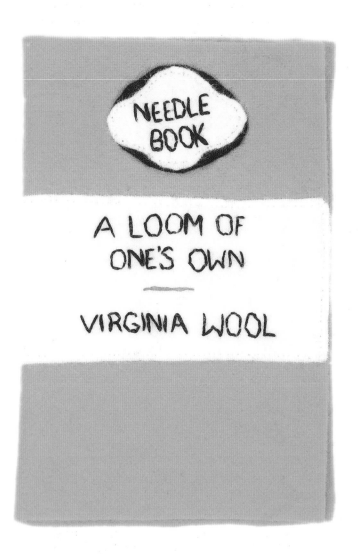

Tools

~ dressmakers' pins
~ sewing needle
~ scissors
~ pinking shears
  (optional)

Materials

~ approx 23cm x 23cm of white felt
~ approx 23cm x 23cm of orange felt
~ approx 5cm x 5cm of black felt
~ embroidery thread in black and orange
~ white sewing thread

What to do

1. Cut out a rectangle measuring 5cm x 20cm from the white felt – this will be used as the title strip of the book.
2. Fold in half. With the fold to your left, faintly mark out in pencil the title, A LOOM OF ONE'S OWN, and the author, VIRGINIA WOOL.
3. Cut a length, about 40cm, of black embroidery thread, and split the strands in half: two lengths of three strands. With one three-strand piece, make a knot at one end and thread the other end through the needle. You're now ready to start stitching the letters: use a backstitch and follow the pencil lines.
4. In orange embroidery thread, sew a couple of stitches between the name of the book and the author.
5. From the remaining white felt, cut out an oval measuring 2.5cm x 5cm, then cut it into a round-edged diamond shape. Pencil on the words NEEDLE BOOK and stitch in black embroidery thread as before (fig A).
6. Cut a slightly larger oval shape from the black felt.
7. Cut out a rectangle from the orange felt measuring 15cm x 20cm for the book cover.

8. Pin the white title piece in the centre of the orange rectangle. Using the white thread, sew a running stitch all around the edges of the white panel.
9. Place the black oval above the title panel, in the centre. Pin the white "NEEDLE BOOK" piece on top of the black oval, and stitch around the white shape as before.
10. Using pinking shears if you have them, cut out a rectangle of white felt measuring 13cm x 18cm.
11. Open up the orange book, and pin the white felt in the centre.
12. Along the middle of the white felt, where the book folds, sew the white felt to the orange with a straight line of stitches (fig B) – the smaller the stitches, the neater the look. Fold in half, and stow your needles away safely.

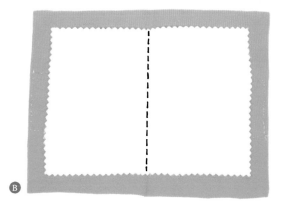

Seleena Laverne Daye likes to refer to herself as a Felt Artist, which means she likes to spend her days in her closet-cum-studio making things out of felt. She also likes to refer to herself as a professional zinester, being co-producer of biannual craft zine *Sugar Paper; 20 Things To Make And Do*. When not distracted by her cat, tap dancing and collecting bits of tat, the things she makes can be found on her blog: *www.sugarpapergang.blogspot.com*.

Interview with Aesthetic Outburst's Abbey Hendrickson

What are your earliest crafting memories? My parents are both very creative and have always encouraged my creative pursuits. As a child, I also had a babysitter who let us draw all over her basement walls. I still keep in touch with her and, when I went to visit a few years ago, all of the drawings that I had made when I was four years old were still there. It was kind of magical to see walls absolutely covered in marks I made 30 years ago! That creative freedom had a tremendous impact on me.

When and why did you start up your blog? Aesthetic Outburst started as a way to keep in touch with family and friends when I was pregnant with our first baby. In many ways it remains that; it's just grown a bit. We've moved a few times, finished college, had two babies, and now I'm a full-time blogger and artist living in a tiny town in upstate New York. It's still hard for me to believe that anyone besides my mum wants to see what I make.

Where do you craft? There's a room in our house that I've claimed as a studio, though, quite honestly, I use our dining-room table more than any other space. My husband and I have just started renovating a 150-year-old farmhouse and have plans to build studios in an outbuilding (my husband is also an artist). I'll be curious to see if the dining-room table still wins out once I have an official studio space.

What is the most amazing thing you have ever made? I absolutely love to make costumes for our two babies. When they're flying around the yard dressed as owls or flower bouquets, it makes me incandescently happy.

What is your biggest crafting disaster? Disasters happen almost every day. Truly. That's all part of the fun, isn't it? I live for the disasters because you never know when one is going to set you on a path to something really good; something you couldn't have imagined without almost complete catastrophe.

What is your dream craft project? Oh, good question! I seem to have so many dream craft projects that it's difficult to decide. I'd like to sew a quilt completely by hand, or knit something incredible. First on the agenda is learning how to knit.

Do you feel part of a craft movement or scene? I definitely consider myself to be part of an online community of crafters, artists and bloggers. I certainly don't think I'm doing anything revolutionary though: most of my days are spent hanging out at home, making things, talking about making things and hoping others will make things.

Where does your craft inspiration come from? It sounds so clichéd, but inspiration is everywhere. I thought it would be more difficult to find inspiration when we moved to my rural hometown, but the move has had the opposite effect. There just aren't as many distractions here. Life is quieter, which allows ideas to be louder. The blogging community is also a constant source of inspiration, and I'm also a bit of a book and magazine addict. I particularly love craft books from the 1950s to the 1970s. And just meandering through a craft store on any given day can spark so many ideas.

Abbey Hendrickson's **Abstract Cubes**

Colourful, wooden blocks to occupy children – and distracted office workers.

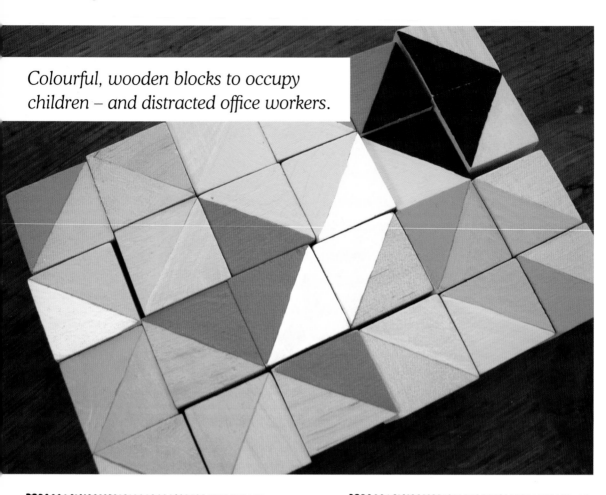

Tools

~ ruler
~ eraser
~ fine sandpaper
~ paintbrushes
~ old milk carton lids to hold paint

If you are cutting your own blocks, you'll also need:

~ junior hacksaw
~ clamps
~ medium-grade sandpaper

Materials

~ 24 wooden cubes – available at craft shops – in any size (these are 2cm x 2cm), or a length of square-ended wood to cut your own blocks
~ acrylic paint in nine colors – this example uses turquoise, pink, yellow, light blue, red, orange, black, white and grey

What to do

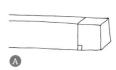

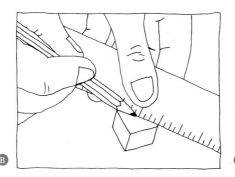

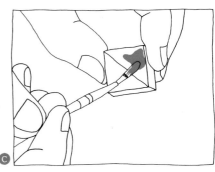

1. If you have ready-bought blocks, skip to step 4. If you are making your own blocks, measure the width of your square-ended wood and mark this measurement along its length. So, if the wood is 2cm x 2cm, mark a line across the wood 2cm up from the end, and at a right angle on the long edge (fig A).
2. Clamp the wood onto an appropriate surface (a workbench is ideal) and saw along the line.

3. Repeat steps 1 and 2 to create 24 blocks, and sand well with the medium-grade paper.
4. Inspect the wooden cubes and find the smoothest side of each. Position the cubes smoothest side up.
5. Use a pencil and ruler to draw a diagonal line from corner to corner on each cube (fig B).
6. If you are feeling very organised, you can make a chart of which colours to paint where. Otherwise, select a cube and paint in one triangle (fig C). Set this cube aside to dry and continue painting one triangle on the remaining cubes.
7. You can leave some cubes with just one triangle painted, but if you want to add colour to the other side, let the first triangle of paint dry first.
8. Leave all of the cubes to dry completely; then rub out any visible pencil marks.
9. Use fine sandpaper to sand away any excess paint over the edges.

Abbey Hendrickson is an artist and blogger living happily in Owego, New York, with her husband and their two babies. She has a background in drawing, book-making and printmaking, and is an enthusiastic crafter. The majority of Abbey's days are spent with her children, pretending to be a superhero, unicorn or robot. In the wee hours, she also writes a popular daily lifestyle blog called Aesthetic Outburst. *aestheticoutburst.blogspot.com, www.etsy.com/shop/hownowdesign.*

Lery's **Spoon Pendant**

By Sarah Jones

Spoon bending minus the psychic bit – use a hammer instead.

Tools
- ~ hammer
- ~ chopping board
- ~ steel wool, grade 2 or 3
- ~ protective gloves (for handling steel wool)
- ~ cigarette lighter

Materials
- ~ spoon with a decorative handle
- ~ approx 40cm length of ribbon, or silver chain and clasp
- ~ nail varnish
- ~ newspaper

What to do

1. Rub the steel wool over the front part of the handle and the convex part (at the back) of the spoon's bowl, to create a matt look.
2. At a point about 2cm up from the bowl of the spoon, use your hands to bend the handle backwards as far as you can (fig A).
3. Place the chopping board on a solid surface. Open up the newspaper so that one side covers the board, and place the spoon on top, with the bend in the spoon close to the fold in the newspaper.
4. Fold the other side of the newspaper over the bent spoon, and holding the spoon bowl with one hand and the hammer in the other (fig B), press the handle down firmly to tighten the bend and curve the handle over the convex bowl of the spoon.
5. Paint the decorative part of the spoon handle with nail varnish in a colour of your choice. When it has dried, rub over the painted area with the steel wool so that the pattern comes into relief.
6. Cut the ribbon to length with diagonal edges and carefully singe the ends with the lighter to prevent fraying. Fasten the ribbon to the spoon with a cow hitch knot. To make the knot, double over the ribbon and hold it between your thumb and index finger so that a loop sticks out at the top. With your other hand, put your thumb and index finger through the loop from back to front; pinch the two strands of ribbon hanging down (fig C), and pull them through the loop.

7. Remove your thumb from the knot, and slide the spoon handle into the same place. Tighten the knot around the spoon, and tie a bow to attach it around the neck.

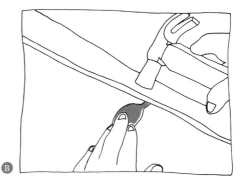

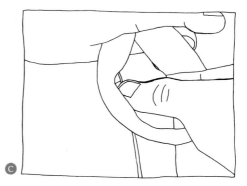

Sarah Jones lives in east London and gets her creative inspiration from the diversity, momentum and dynamism of her surrounds. She studied silversmithing and uses these skills to refashion unwanted stainless-steel cutlery into jewellery: pendants are made from spoons, earrings from fork tines and brooches from various cutlery handles. *www.lery.co.uk.*

The Hipster Headdress

By Victoria Woodcock and Dave Hillier

Feather your head for the festival season.

Tools

~ dressmakers' pins
~ sewing needle
~ thimble
~ piece of thick cardboard or spatula
~ pegs

Materials

~ 35cm x 7cm piece of buckram
~ approx 30cm of 0.5cm-1cm-thick elastic
~ 36cm x 8cm piece of felt
~ selection of feathers
~ sequins, ribbon, beads, wool, embroidery thread etc to decorate
~ sewing thread in same colour as felt
~ all-purpose glue

What to do

1. Cut out the pieces of felt (36cm x 8cm) and buckram (35cm x 7cm). Fold over the buckram lengthways. Then unfold, leaving a crease. Place on a piece of newspaper so you don't get glue on the table.

2. Above the crease, position feathers, bit of ribbon etc – anything you want to stick out of your headdress. Once you have your design sorted, glue the elements in place. To do so, squeeze a small amount of glue onto the feather stem or ribbon, leave for around 30 seconds for the glue to go tacky, then hold onto the buckram until secure. Repeat for each item, then leave to dry for 10 minutes.

3. Squiggle glue over the second half of the buckram, then smooth over with a stub of cardboard or spatula. Fold over the buckram again, trapping the feathers etc in the middle. Use pegs to hold it in place, nestling them next to the feather stems to ensure they are securely trapped (fig A). Leave to dry.

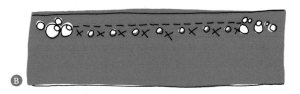

B

A

4. The felt strip will wrap round the buckram, so while you're waiting for the buckram to dry you can decorate the top half that will show on the front. Use a big needle and stitch wool yarn in stripes or crosses; use a small needle and cotton thread to sew on sequins and beads; glue on strips of ribbon and gems (fig B).

5. Set the felt band to one side. On the buckram headdress, pin one end of the elastic to the inside, close to the short edge. Sew securely in place – use the thimble when sewing through the tough buckram. Hold the headdress on your head and stretch the elastic around the back. Pinch the elastic where it joins the other side of the buckram. Remove from your head and pin this "pinched point" to the other side of the buckram; sew to secure. Trim any excess elastic.

6. Squiggle glue onto the front of the headdress, on the buckram, and smear evenly all over. Starting at one end, carefully position the felt onto the band, stretching it out gently as you go across. Smooth over with your finger to check it's stuck down all over with no creases.

7. Apply glue as in step 6 to the back of the headdress band. Fold over the remainder of the felt tightly and stick it onto the back band. Leave to dry.

> **TIP**
> For an extra flourish to your feathers, hang a string of beads and buttons from the band.

Seaside Sisters' **Bunting**

By Gillian Elam, Linda White and Xtina Lamb

Bunting is everywhere these days; make yours the most creative of them all.

Materials

- ~ pieces of fabric at least 20cm x 20cm (any type of fabric is fine)
- ~ approx 2m strip of 25mm-wide bias binding (for eight flags) – a trim designed to be folded around a fabric edge
- ~ smaller scraps of fabric
- ~ sewing threads
- ~ spare bits and bobs of haberdashery for decoration, such as pom-pom or lace trim, beads and felt
- ~ fabric glue (optional)
- ~ fabric paint (optional)

Tools

- ~ dressmakers' pins
- ~ sewing needle
- ~ ruler
- ~ tailors' chalk, or pencil
- ~ scissors
- ~ iron
- ~ sewing machine (optional)

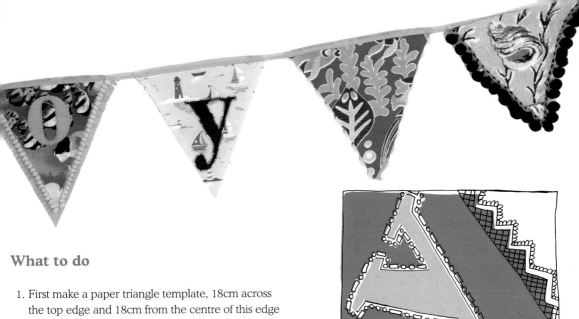

What to do

1. First make a paper triangle template, 18cm across the top edge and 18cm from the centre of this edge to the point.
2. Gather together the fabrics you want to use and put them all in a line to see which sit well together. Decide on the combination before you begin cutting.
3. Pin the template onto the fabric and cut out your flag shape 1cm from the template edge. To make plain bunting, skip to step 8.

4. You can decorate the flags to spell out a message or name, with letters made from fabric scraps, felt, beads and paint. Draw out the letters, or print in an enlarged font from the computer, and cut out to make paper stencils.
5. To make letters like the "a" and the "o" of this "ahoy" bunting, pin the letter templates felt and cut out. Pin the felt letters to the centre of the flag and attach with a running stitch all around the edges of the shape (fig A). Use matching or contrasting colour threads for different effects. You can also experiment with different stitches – backstitch, blanket stitch, overhand stitch – or just glue the letters on. Use it sparingly, though; if too much glue is applied it will show through the fabric.
6. The "h" and the "y" on this example are painted on in fabric paint. To do this, draw around the letter stencils on the flags with a pen or tailors' chalk (fig B). Place the flags on top of some newspaper, and then brush on fabric paint. Leave the paint to dry according to the instructions; then you can add a fancy edge. Sew around the letter in sparkly thread, or make a beaded border (fig C). To sew the beads on, use regular sewing thread and a thin needle to do a running stitch, but every time you bring the needle to the right side of the fabric, pop on a bead.

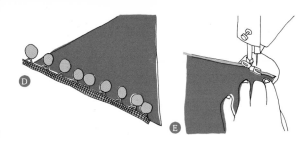

7. The flags without letters can be adorned too. Add fabric shapes or iron-on motifs such as the anchor.

8. Each flag can be finished in different ways. The "a", for example, is "bagged out" with another piece of fabric on the back. To do this you will need another unadorned triangle. Place the two flags right sides together, with the letter in the middle, and sew along the two diagonal edges 1cm in from the edge with a running stitch (or with a machine). Leave the top edge open and turn the shape right side out. Iron.

9. Attaching rickrack, lace, or pom-poms to the diagonal edges adds another dimension. With the "y" and the red-patterned flags, this is done in the same way as step 8. On one of the triangles, however, draw lines 1cm in from the diagonal sides (where you will be sewing). Place the trim along these lines, with about 4mm of the trim over the line towards the edge of the fabric, (or with pom-poms, all of the braid on the fabric-edge side of the line), and the bit you want to be seen facing inwards (fig D). Then place the second triangle on top, right sides facing together, and pin carefully so that the trim is trapped in place. Sew as in step 8 and turn right side out.

10. Alternatively, you can sew bias binding or braid along the rough fabric edges of the triangle. Trim the diagonal edges by 1cm so they are the same size as the backed flags from steps 8 and 9. Bias binding can be folded round the edge (as in the turquoise flag with pom-poms) and sewn down with a running stitch or a machine straight stitch: stop sewing before you reach the point of the triangle and carefully fold the binding round the point (fig E). Then sew to the point; and if using a sewing machine, lift the foot with the needle in the point, and swivel the fabric to continue up the other side.

11. To edge in the same way as the anchor flag, simply sew on the braid, folding neatly at the point. You can then hand-sew ribbon on the back to cover the rough edge of the fabric.

12. For a fancy felt-edged flag like the "o", place the fabric flag on a piece of felt and cut out a felt triangle that is slightly bigger than the fabric one. Position a trim, such as the pink pom-pom braid, in between the fabric and felt, and pin. Sew straight lines along the diagonal edges of the fabric, going through the trim and the felt too (fig F). Snip into the felt edging with regularly spaced slits to form a fringe.

13. When all the flags are complete, press them with an iron and lay them out, deciding how much space you want between them. Measure out a length of bias binding to sew across the top, with an extra 30cm or so at each end for tying. Iron the bias binding so it is folded in half lengthways, and use it to sandwich the top edges of the flags. Pin in place and stitch carefully along the bottom edge of the bias binding, making sure you sew through all the top edges of the flags.

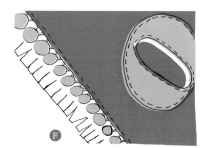

Gillian Elam of Fabric Nation, Linda White of Handmade to Measure and Xtina Lamb of Printed Wonders are the Seaside Sisters; a collective that make and sell handmade textile and paper goods, and run bunting, printmaking and textile workshops. The three designer-makers are united by a love for colourful, original mid-century fabrics, bunting and all things to do with the seaside. They like bunting a lot.... *www.seasidesisters.co.uk*.

Chocolate Creative's **Transfer T-Shirts**

By Margarita Lorenzo

Get drawn in!

Materials

~ T-shirt
~ A4 T-shirt transfer paper (there are two types of paper – one for light coloured fabric and one for dark – make sure you choose the right one).
~ colouring pens, paints or crayons
~ colouring book (optional)

Tools

~ scissors
~ scanner, or digital camera
~ iron
~ colour printer

What to do

1. Draw a picture with children of anything at all, using any medium they like. If they are really young, choose a picture in a colouring book and let them loose on it
2. Scan your drawing or, if you don't have a scanner, take a clear close-up photograph and upload it to your computer.
3. If you have any experience with a photo-retouching program, such as Photoshop, clean up the image and resize it so that it fills the transfer paper nicely. If the image has any words, you need to flip the image too, otherwise it will be backwards.
4. Print the image onto the transfer paper and cut out (fig A).
5. Iron the T-shirt to make the surface smooth. Then place the image face down, and iron the back for about four minutes, moving the iron constantly. Let the T-shirt cool down for a minute and then peel the back off the paper.

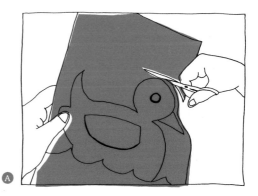

Ⓐ

Margarita Lorenzo is the designer behind Chocolate Creative, a handmade homeware brand based in south London. Craft has always been a big part of her life, so after many years working as a graphic designer, she decided to explore new ways of applying her passion for textiles and her design knowledge to her own creative business. *www.chocolatecreative.co.uk, chocolatecreative.blogspot.com.*

Interview with Merrimaking's Meg Tait and Harri Symes

What are your earliest crafting memories?

M: When I was really young, my friend and I were obsessed with raising money for animal charities, so we used to make bookmarks. I lived in a community at the time so we used to sell them to everyone who lived there. I also remember being really into making puppets with jointed limbs, using those butterfly clips.

H: I used to make cardigans for My Little Pony.

How did Merrimaking come about?

M: It was the summer of 2009. We'd finished university and were working at festivals, all the while wearing the animal hoods that we'd been making. We thought the hoods would be a good way to make some money on site - so that we could afford to be at a couple more festivals - and we decided to make a few to sell and see how it went. First we went to Green Man, then we went to Bestival, and we just got really great feedback. So we kept making them, and it has carried on funding our fun.

H: This is the whole premise behind what we do; that we didn't have much money. That's why we set up the Swap Shop. Instead of paying in actual money, people sometimes send us what they value at £25 - something that we need, like fabric. We needed an iron, and we got one through the Swap Shop. We've also swapped hoods for festival tickets, and lifts to and from them. It's so satisfying that there's no money involved and because we get to use reclaimed fabrics, people get something more unique.

How does Merrimaking work between the two of you?

H: We both sort of do everything. At the moment, Meg is designing the website and I'm really enjoying making the unusual hoods that we get commissioned to make. The company stuff really comes in our lunch breaks, when we sit and chat, and come up with ideas. We now employ two friends who help with the pattern-cutting and sewing.

What's the best thing you've ever made?

H: I always forget about the stuff I've made; then when I clear out my room I find the most phenomenal amount of stuff that Meg and I have made for each other. The other day I found the most amazing jumper. We had two pet rats when we lived in Brighton and they used to sit on our shoulders, so the jumper has two rats, made out of fabric, sewn onto the shoulders, and one of the tails comes all the way down the front.

M: I graduated from university hanging from the ceiling in a horse costume. I'd made the hoist myself, and it didn't break and embarrass me, so I'm pretty fond of it for that.

At the moment I'm wearing some trousers that Harri made me for Christmas. They're made of two pairs of pyjama trousers, cut in half and sewn together down the middle. Pretty brilliant!

H: About half the stuff we wear we made for each other.

And the worst thing you've ever made?
H: This is going to sound really strange, and it's not exactly the worst, but someone commissioned me to make a Pterodactyl hood, and when I flattened it out, it looked like a vagina!

Were do you get your craft inspiration?
M: At the moment, we are completely in awe of a collective called Jiggery Pokery. We only recently came across them, and then, randomly, we met them three days later. They're two women from London, and some of their stuff is really high end, but it's all really fun. [www.jiggerypokery.biz.]

H: We're also really inspired by festivals, such as Secret Garden Party. Everyone really dresses up. Everyone is at their best; at their most creative.

Do you look at any specific websites/books/magazines for inspiration or practical tips?
M: Not for practical tips, no - we just make it up and each time the designs get better. We're definitely still learning, but I've learnt a lot without realising it, just from trial and error. Sometimes, though, all you need is Google. I image-searched how to cast off when I was knitting the other day and, of course, someone had drawn some instructions! Who are these people? They're endlessly helpful.

What is your dream craft project?
H: Well, someone suggested that we make a corgi hood for the queen… And then we actually made it! But I can't see her wearing it somehow.

M: I'd like to work on something really over the top; like, maybe, making the outfits for the Cirque Du Soleil.

Where do you craft?
M: We have a really fantastic studio in Nottingham. It's in my favourite building of all time - an old, and massive, lace mill full of art studios and small industries. The ceilings are high and the windows are huge, with old metal frames. I love it.

Do you feel part of a craft scene or movement?
M: There's definitely a strong and interesting artistic community around us, and within our friendship group. We have one friend who runs a brilliant company called Spinsters Emporium [www.spinstersemporium.co.uk] which is craft based, and we are surrounded by illustrators and fine artists. It's a good balance.

Merrimaking's **Animal Ears for Cyclists**

By Meg Tait and Harri Symes

Make drivers pay attention with furry ears for your bike helmet!

Tools

~ dressmakers' pins
~ sewing needle, or sewing machine

Materials

~ 12cm x 48cm of fake-fur fabric
~ shoelace
~ sewing thread

What to do

1. Cut out four squares of fake-fur fabric measuring 12cm x 12cm.
2. Place one square face down and fold over 1cm along one edge. Pin; then sew a straight stitch with a machine or hand sew a running stitch close to the top edge of the fold (fig A). Repeat for the remaining three squares.
3. Place one square of fabric fur side up, with the fold at the bottom edge closest to you. Place another square on top, with the fold in the same place, but this time with the fur side facing down. Pin together and draw an arched ear shape in pen, staying at least 1cm from the fabric edge (fig B). Sew along the line. Repeat with the other two squares.
4. Cut around the arch shapes 1cm from the stitching. Turn the ears fur-side out.
5. Along the bottom edge of the ear, pinch at the middle point between the two seams, and pull apart (fig C).
6. Find the centre of the shoelace. Place the "pinched point" of one ear 5cm-6cm away from the centre point. Hand-sew the shoelace to the ear here. Repeat with the second ear on the other side of the centre point (fig D).
7. Attach the other pinched points of the ears 8cm further along the lace from the first points (fig E).
8. To affix the ears to your bike helmet, tie the lace through any gap in the plastic, as tightly as possible; or you can tie them straight round your head.

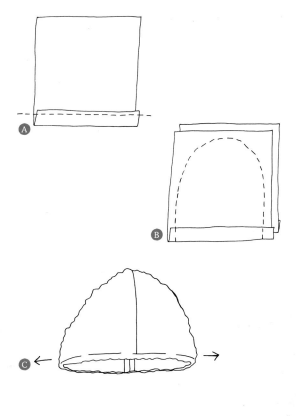

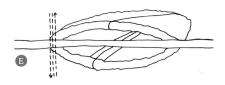

Meg Tait and Harri Symes met at university, where they studied Fine Art and Philosophy and made and wore animal hoods. They played in them, cycled in them, learnt in them and kept their pet rat warm in them. In 2009, they finished uni and decided to make more hoods to sell at festivals as a means to fund some fun, and Merrimaking began: a design house dedicated to playful, bespoke pieces. *www.merrimaking.co.uk.*

Urban Cross Stitch's **Invaders Tote Bag**

By Phil Davison

Perfectly pixilated for cross-stitch, invading aliens are retro geek chic.

Tools

~ dressmakers' pins
~ size 20 embroidery needle
~ scissors
~ ruler or measuring tape
~ tailors' chalk, or pencil
~ embroidery hoop (optional)
~ sewing machine, or sewing needle

Materials

~ 23cm x 26cm piece of 14-count soluble cross-stitch canvas, such as by DMC
~ embroidery floss in the six colours outlined on the chart (p 238)
~ approx 2m of 2cm-wide black canvas tape
~ 45cm x 100cm black cotton canvas fabric
~ black and white sewing threads

Skills

~ cross-stitch

What to do

1. Cut a rectangular piece of black cotton canvas measuring 45cm x 100cm; this is the main body of the tote bag.
2. Pin a hem on both the short edges. To do so, fold over about 1cm of fabric, and iron flat. Fold over the fabric again, by about 2cm this time, to hide the rough edge, and press again. Pin in place.
3. These hemmed edges will be at the opening of the tote, and the long edges will be folded in half to form the side seams. Position the 23cm x 26cm piece of soluble canvas on one half of the bag, on the right side of the fabric. The shorter edge should be at the top, about 8cm from the hemmed edge, and with equal amounts of fabric to either side. Pin in place then tack (sew a big, loose running stitch) the soluble canvas to the tote body around the edge, and diagonally across the middle (fig A).
4. Position the tote body/soluble canvas into an embroidery hoop. Using the chart template on page 238, find the centre of the chart and the centre of the soluble canvas and start cross-stitching the design. Cut a 50cm length of embroidery thread, and separate the strands into three sets of two. Use two strands of embroidery floss for all stitches.
5. Each square on the chart is a full cross-stitch, while each symbol has a corresponding thread colour – as per the key at the bottom of the chart. Read the pattern carefully to make sure you are using the right colour for each stitch. It is also helpful to colour in, with a highlighter pen, the symbols on the chart that you have stitched.

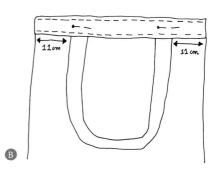

6. When the Invaders motif is complete, remove the tacking stitches and carefully trim away the excess soluble canvas around the cross-stitching.
7. Cut two pieces of black canvas tape to form the handles. The length is up to you, but a good average length is around 1m per strap.
8. On the reverse side of the tote bag body, tuck one end of one strap under the hem, approx 11cm in from the edge; pin in place. Position the other end of the strap approx 11cm in from the other side, making sure the tape isn't twisted. Repeat at the bottom hemmed edge with the remaining strap.
9. With the strap hanging down against the body of the bag, sew two straight lines to secure the hem and the strap – one 2mm from the top edge and the other just up from the bottom of the hem (fig B). Use the machine and work with the right side of the fabric facing up toward you (and the hem and the strap at the back). You can mark out the line just up from the bottom of the hem in tailors' chalk on the front to make sure you catch the fold at the back. Repeat at the other hemmed edge.

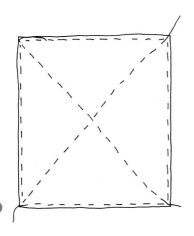

"My grandmother gave me a needle and a pattern and taught me to cross-stitch. The patterns, while intricate, were very twee."

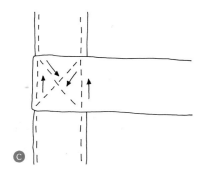

C

10. Flip the straps up over the hem, and secure with machine stitching. Again working on the front of the fabric, sew over the strap along the top line of stitching, diagonally down to the bottom line of stitching, across this, and then back up diagonally forming a cross (fig C).

11. Fold the tote bag body in half so that the two hemmed edges meet and the right sides are touching. Pin, then sew a straight line down either side, 1cm from the fabric edge. Turn the tote right side out.

12. Now to dissolve the soluble canvas. Put the stitched fabric in a bowl with a large volume of hot soapy water (between 40°C and 50°C), and let it soak for five to 10 minutes, stirring gently from time to time. The soluble canvas will melt and disappear. Rinse with plenty of hot water, then hang out to dry.

Phil Davison was born in Belfast, studied pattern-cutting at Central St Martins College of Art and Design in London, and has been bringing his "Cupcakes! Cocktails! & Cross Stitch!" nights to London clubs since 2008, with the invention of Urban Cross Stitch. Now a thriving business, his patterns are based on popular art such as Banksy and 1980s children's entertainment characters, taking cross-stitching to a new level. *www.urban-cross-stitch.com*.

Heart Zeena's
Birdie Lavender Bag / Pincushion

By Zeena Shah

Something to tweet about!

Tools

~ dressmakers' pins
~ scissors
~ tailors' chalk, or pencil
~ iron
~ sewing machine (optional)

Materials

~ two pieces of 15cm x 15cm cotton fabric. This version uses one plain square for the bird design and one patterned square at the back
~ dried lavender or polyester toy stuffing for the pin cushion (or make your own stuffing from a chopped-up item of old clothing)
~ 16cm of thin ribbon to create a hanging loop (for the lavender bag)
~ sheet of paper
~ fabric paint pen (optional)

What to do

1. Copy the bird template on page 229 onto paper and cut out. On the back of one of the fabric squares, draw around the template.
2. If you want to create the bird design with a fabric pen, now is the time to do it. Lay the plain fabric square right side facing up on a few sheets of newspaper. In pencil or tailors' chalk, faintly draw a bird outline an equal distance (about 1cm) within the template shape; add an eye and a beak, then map out lines of dashes, dots and little hearts to create a pattern. Draw over the lines with a fabric pen and leave to dry. Cover the design with newspaper and iron to fix according to the pen instructions (fig A).
3. Place the two pieces of fabric together with the right sides facing. If you want to create a hanging loop, cut a 16cm length of ribbon, double it over and pin it between the fabrics at the centre top of the bird shape, with the two ribbon ends sticking out beyond the template lines at the top of the bird (fig B).

4. Pin evenly all the way around the shape. Following the pencil line, sew around the bird shape, leaving a 5cm gap. You can use a straight stitch on a sewing machine or sew it by hand using a running stitch (fig C).

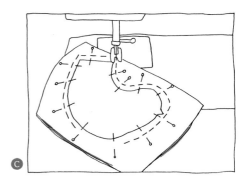

5. Remove the pins and trim any unwanted threads. Cut around the shape 1cm away from stitching.
6. Cut out V-shaped notches around any curves (fig D) to allow the fabric to move.
7. Turn the shape right side out and press using a medium to hot iron.
8. Fill the shape with dried lavender stuffing or polyester, depending on whether you are making a lavender bag or a pincushion.
9. Sew up the gap by hand as neatly as you can, using a whipstitch.

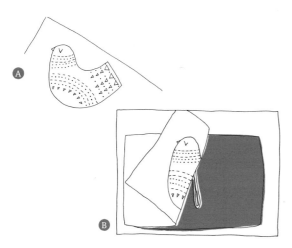

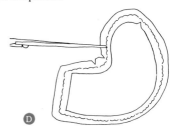

Zeena Shah studied printed textile design at Chelsea School of Art and Design and has since worked in both the fashion and interiors textile industry. In 2009, inspired by her love of paper-cutting, printing, birds and hearts, she launched her own label, Heart Zeena – a collection of handmade silkscreen-printed textiles for the home. Zeena also runs a programme of craft workshops, inspiring people to get stitching. *www.zeenashah.com, www.heartzeena.blogspot.com.*

Coralie Sleap's **Barrel Bag**

More challenging that making a tote bag – and a great project to learn how to put in a zip.

Tools

~ dressmakers' pins
~ sewing needle
~ tape measure
~ tailors' chalk, or a pencil
~ scissors
~ pinking shears (optional)
~ iron
~ plate with a 17cm-18cm diameter, or a set of compasses
~ sewing machine

Materials

~ approx 60cm of any fabric that's not too lightweight or too thick
~ 45cm x 8cm strip of lightweight fabric to support the zip
~ 35cm zip
~ 2m of webbing or fabric tape for the handles, about 2.5cm wide
~ sewing thread to match the fabric

What to do

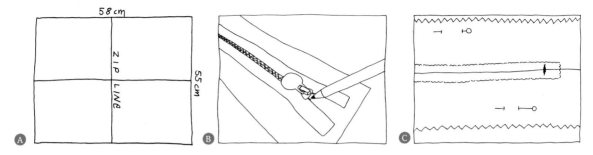

1. Measure and cut out a 58cm x 55cm rectangle for the body of the bag. Then draw around the plate twice on the remaining fabric and cut out to make the two ends of the bag (1.5cm seam allowances are included in the measurements).
2. Measure out the 45cm x 8cm strip of lightweight fabric to support the zip. Use pinking shears to cut out if you have them; otherwise, cut out 2cm around the rectangle and hem the long edges. To hem, fold over the edges by about 1cm; press with an iron. Then fold them over by the same amount again; press and sew through all layers with a straight stitch about 8mm from the fabric edge.
3. On the main body fabric, mark out the centre point of each edge and join up with lines across, in tailors' chalk or a pencil, to form a cross on the right side of the fabric (fig A).
4. The 55cm line across the centre is the zip line. Lay the 45cm x 8cm piece of fabric face down (right sides together) centred over the zip line and pin. Redraw the centre lines over this fabric.
5. Lay the zip in the centre of the zip line and mark where the teeth begin and end (fig B).

6. Remove the zip. Draw a line 5mm from the centre zip line on either side. At a right angle to these lines, and 5mm out from where the zip teeth begin and end, draw two short lines to form a rectangle.
7. Machine stitch around this rectangle with a straight stitch along the lines (fig C).
8. Leaving 1cm at either end, cut down the centre of the rectangle, along the zip line, through both layers of fabric.
9. Snip diagonally into the corners of the rectangle (fig D), taking care not to cut into the stitches.
10. Remove the pins and turn the small piece of fabric through the opening to the inside (fig E). Press it flat.
11. With the wrong side of the fabric facing up, centre the closed zip along the opening, and pin in place. If you have one, change the foot on your machine to a zip foot, and sew around the zip through the zip tape and the fabric, about 1.5cm away from the teeth. Zip: done!
12. Now for the handles: 8cm from the centre line that intersects the zip, draw a line on each side going right the way across the zip to each end of the fabric. On these lines, mark 10cm down from the zip on each side.

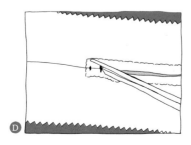

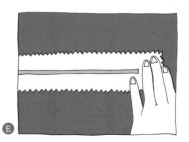

13. Cut the webbing/fabric tape in half. Place one end at the edge of the fabric and pin it along the line you've just drawn up to the mark 10cm from the zip. Then match up the other end of the webbing with the fabric edge and the other line on the same side of the zip, making sure the webbing is not twisted, and pin from the fabric edge to the 10cm mark. There will be a loop left for the handle (fig F).

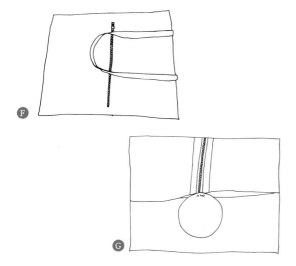

14. Sew along each side of the webbing to secure (don't sew past the 10cm point). You can sew a square with a cross in it at each end nearest the zip to add strength.
15. Attach the other handle to the opposite side.
16. Now to add the end circles. Fold each of them in half along the grain of the fabric. Mark out the centre line on the wrong side of the fabric. Cut a small notch (V-shaped snip) at the centre line on each end, and a couple more on each side.
17. With right sides together, position the circle to one end of the bag, with the top notch on the centre line of the circle and the zip line matching up (fig G). Pin.

18. Curve the straight fabric edge around the circle, matching up the fabric edges and pinning as you go, 1.5cm in from the edge. Stop at the other end of the centre line on the circle. Then fold the fabric on the other side of the zip around the other half of the circle, pinning the right sides of the fabric together in the same way.
19. Tack (sew a rough running stitch by hand) around the circle. Make sure the stitches join up across the bottom of the circle. Then sew around the circle on the sewing machine, 1.5cm from the fabric edge.
20. Repeat steps 17-19 at the other end of the bag.
21. Open the zip (or your bag will be sewn shut!) and pin the long edges of fabric together at the bottom of the bag, right sides together. Sew a straight line joining up the stitches at the bottom of the circle at either end.
22. Press the seams open, pushing the tip of the iron in between the two seam allowances, and turn bag right side out. Fill with stuff!

Coralie Sleap is the co-owner of DRINK, SHOP & DO, a café bar and shop in Kings Cross, London, that hosts lots of interesting and inspiring nights – some crafty; some downright silly; all lots of fun. www.drinkshopdo.com.

Felicity Hall's
Bird on a Branch Needlepoint

A thoroughly modern take on tapestry.

Tools

~ size 22 tapestry needle
~ piece of plywood measuring at least 40cm x 40cm
~ some rustproof nails or carpet tacks
~ atomiser spray
~ embroidery frame, such as a 45cm x 30cm Elbesee Easy Clip frame (optional)
~ hammer

Materials

~ 35cm x 35cm piece of 14hpi (14 holes per inch) needlework canvas, such as Zweigart mono canvas
~ 4-ply tapestry wool in black (20m), white (15m), grey (60m), metallic gold (8m)
~ masking tape

What to do

1. It's always best to make a shade card before you begin a needlepoint design. Just take a strip of card and punch some holes in it; then tie a small length of each wool colour to each hole and label it with the shade number and corresponding chart symbol.

2. Photocopy all four parts of the design on pages 234-237 and place them together. Trace the outline of the design onto a piece of scrap paper and cut out. Set the template aside for when you come to block the finished piece (where you stretch the canvas into the correct shape).

3. Fold masking tape around the edges of the canvas to prevent it from fraying. It's up to you whether to use a frame or not. Some stitchers prefer to, as it leaves two hands free and stops the canvas from being distorted by the stitches (although any distortion can be rectified when the canvas is blocked).

4. Time to start stitching! This chart is designed to be worked in tent stitch – a diagonal embroidery stitch that crosses over the intersection of one horizontal (weft) and one vertical (warp) thread of needlepoint canvas. Two versions of the tent stitch are used: the basketweave technique for the background, and continental stitch for the fiddly smaller areas and outlines.

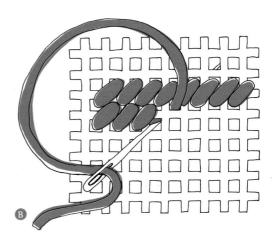

5. Cut a piece of wool roughly 25cm long (short enough to stop it from twisting and tangling while you're stitching). Pick part of the design to work on, say the branch, and follow the chart using a continental tent stitch. Leave a 2.5cm loose length of wool at the back of the canvas (don't knot) and work the first few stitches from right to left (fig A), forming diagonal stitches on the back of the canvas as well as the front, and catching the yarn end in these stitches.

6. Work the next row of stitches from left to right (fig B). Continuing working one row from right to left, and the next from left to right. To fasten off the end of a length of wool, pass it through a horizontal or vertical row of stitches on the back of the canvas and trim off any excess.

7. Work the branch, the bird and the border pattern using the continental tent stitch.

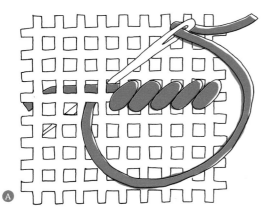

8. Fill in the background areas using the basketweave stitch (as it distorts the canvas less). This is worked in diagonal rows, forming vertical and horizontal stitches at the back. Work the first row downwards diagonally from left to right (fig C), forming vertical stitches at the back, and stitching over the loose length of wool.

9. Work the next row upwards diagonally from right to left (fig D), forming horizontal stitches at the back and slotting like a stepladder in between each of the stitches of the previous row. Repeat the downward and upward rows alternately and fasten off as for the continental stitch.

10. When finished, don't panic if your canvas has slightly distorted: stitched canvas can be dampened, stretched and pulled back into shape. This is called blocking. Lay the completed work face down on the plywood and spray it thoroughly with water. Using the paper template as a guide, stretch the canvas back into its original shape. Start by hammering a nail into the centre of each side and then work outwards towards the corners. Let the needlepoint dry completely – this may take a few days.

11. Remove the nails and frame your handiwork.

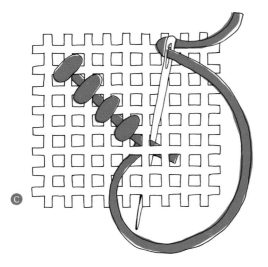

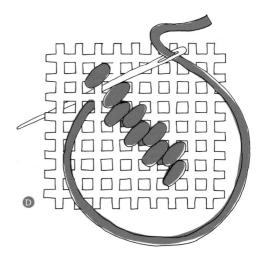

Felicity Hall is passionate about stitching; for her there is nothing more rewarding, or relaxing, than taking the time to sit and make something beautiful from a piece of canvas and some lengths of wool. With her needlepoint kits, she creates contemporary designs that are both fun to stitch and that fit into a modern interior – heirlooms for a future generation to enjoy. *www.felicityhall.co.uk*.

I Heart…'s **See You Soon Card**

By Iona Bruce

What to do

1. Cut a length of embroidery thread approx 30cm-40cm long. Divide the thread in half, so you have two sets with three strands each. Thread the needle with one three-strand piece, and tie a couple of knots at the other end. Place the Aida into the embroidery hoop, and you're ready to go.
2. For the pattern on page 232, the glasses and the corner decorations are worked in cross-stitch. Working from right to left, follow the chart by counting the number of "x"s on the design, and recreating them on the fabric. Remember that the first stitches of the "x" should always slope in the same direction.
3. The SEE YOU SOON is worked in backstitch (work as in normal fabric, using the holes). Follow the chart to stitch your message.
4. Cut around the cross-stitch design, leaving 1cm around the edges.
5. Squirt some glue on the inside of the card, around the edge of the cut-out square.
6. Place the design face down onto the glue and gently move it about until it is lined up straight with the edges of the cut square (fig A).
7. Squirt some more glue onto the card around your design, then fold the panel on the left-hand side of the card onto it. Press down firmly to make sure it sticks – you're ready to write a message!

Tools

~ embroidery hoop, 10cm diameter
~ embroidery needle
~ scissors

Materials

~ 14cm x 14cm square of 14-count white Aida fabric
~ embroidery thread in various colours
~ aperture card with a 68mm x 68mm square cut out (or you can make your own with a craft knife)
~ all-purpose glue

Skills

~ cross-stitch

Ⓐ

Iona Bruce lives in the Highlands of Scotland where she spends her time making handicrafts, organising community projects and preparing crafty workshops that she facilitates around the UK. She is also rather fond of long walks with her headphones on, knitting on the bus and writing letters on her old typewriter. *www.iheartdotdotdot.co.uk*.

Made by Me's **Leather Baby Shoes**

By Beatrice Owen

Just too darn cute for words!

Tools

~ leather sewing needle
~ small safety pin
~ scissors

Materials

~ 15cm x 16cm piece of leather for soles
~ 14cm x 19cm piece of leather for toes
~ 15cm x 19cm piece of leather for heels
~ 80cm of 7mm-wide ribbon
~ 15cm of 7mm-wide elastic
~ sewing thread in matching colours

What to do

1. Copy the sole, toe and heel templates on page 233 twice onto the back of your pieces of leather and cut out along the lines. Set aside one set of pattern pieces and concentrate on one shoe.
2. On the toe and heel leathers, fold over 1cm along the straight edges to make a hem (fig A), and sew a straight line with a running stitch 8mm from the folded edge.
3. Fold each leather piece in half to find the centre line, and mark this on the wrong side of the fabric with a pencil (fig B).

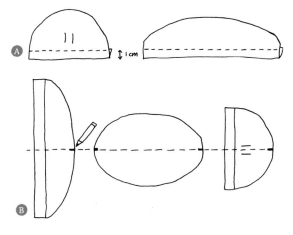

4. On the toe piece, make a small 0.5cm slit either side of the middle of the centre line. The slits should be about 1cm apart.
5. Match up the centre marks at the curved end of the toe and at one end of the sole, placing the right sides together (fig C).

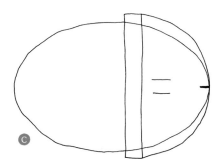

6. Starting at the tip of the toe, carefully sew along the curved edge of the toe to the sole, lining up the edges of leather and sewing in a running stitch about 4mm from the edge. When you reach the edge of the toe section, go back on yourself to the tip, stitching in the gaps. Repeat to attach the other edge, ending at the tip of the toe (fig D).

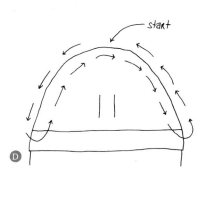

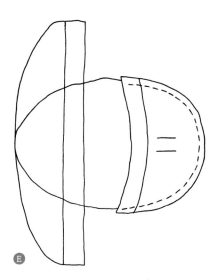

7. Match up the curved edge of the heel to the other end of the sole with the right sides facing each other, again using the centre marks (fig E).

8. In the same way as with the toe, sew the heel to the sole, starting and ending at the back of the heel (fig F). When you get to the sides, you will be sewing over the toe section too: secure the overlapping leather with extra stitches.

7. Cut two 20cm lengths of ribbon and a 7.5cm length of elastic. Sew a piece of ribbon securely to either end of the elastic

8. Attach the safety pin to the length of ribbon/elastic, and thread it through the hem of the heel leather (fig G).

9. Turn the shoe right side out. Pass the ends of the ribbon through the slits in the toe leather from back to front and tie in a bow.

10. Repeat steps 2-9 for the second shoe.

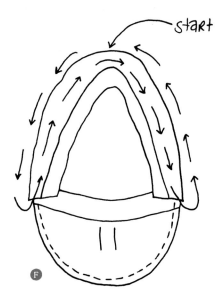

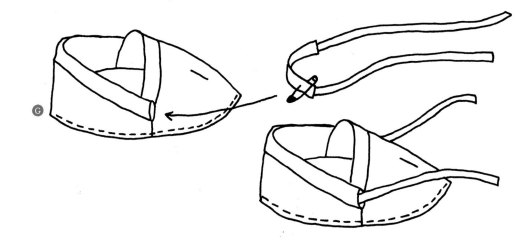

Beatrice Owen is a passionate craftsperson who has taken her love for making things and turned it into a small business, Made by Me. With one-year-old daughter Delilah as inspiration and chief tester, her range of small shoes is the company's main focus, producing soft leather pumps in delicious colours for babies and toddlers, as well as "create your own" packs of ready-cut materials and simple instructions. *www.beatriceowen.com*.

Helen Rawlinson's
Super-Strong Mini Storage Buckets

A home for bits and bobs, mini projects, pens and pencils, cosmetics, toys, keys, phone…

Tools:

~ dressmakers' pins
~ ruler
~ tailors' chalk or pencil
~ scissors
~ iron
~ sewing machine with strong needle for thick sewing

Materials

For one bucket

~ 39cm x 51cm piece of jute
~ 13cm x 51cm piece of patterned medium-weight cotton
~ 24cm x 51cm piece of heavy-duty interfacing (the thicker the better!)
~ cream sewing thread

What to do

1. Measure and draw out two rectangles of jute measuring 26cm x 51cm (for the lining) and 13cm x 51cm (for the base); a 13cm x 51cm rectangle of cotton fabric and a 24cm x 51cm piece of interfacing. Cut out all shapes, keeping the edges as straight as possible.

2. As jute is a loosely woven fabric, it's important to prevent fraying, so set the sewing machine to a zigzag setting, and sew right along all the edges of the two jute panels.

3. Position the patterned panel on top of the 13cm x 51cm jute panel, right sides together, carefully lining up the edges; and pin. Sew along one long length 1cm from the fabric edge.

4. Unfold along the line of stitching so that the two fabrics are one on top of the other. Turn this piece face down on to an ironing board (fig A). Fold over the 1cm seam allowance (both fabrics) on top of the jute, and press.

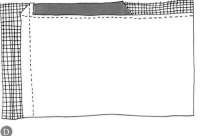

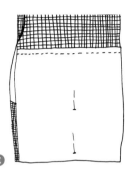

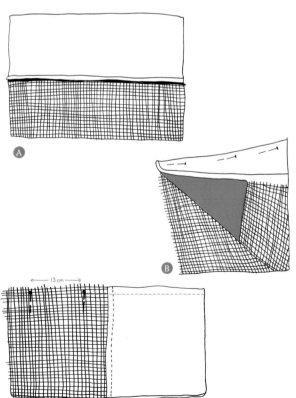

TIP
instead of using jute, you could posh it up with linen, go a bit vintage with some old jeans or add classic lines with striped ticking.

5. On the right side of the joined fabric, sew along the jute next to the join approx 2mm from the seam.

6. Now lay out the larger piece of jute. Place the joined fabric you have just sewn right side down, on top of the jute; then place the interfacing on top of that (fig B). Pin the top edge that has the cotton fabric trapped between the jute and the interfacing. Sew along this top edge 1cm from the fabric edge.

7. Open out the fabric so that the jute is on one side of the seam, and the cotton joined piece and the interfacing on the other. Fold the 1cm seam allowances over towards the jute fabric and press.

8. With the fabric opened out like this, fold it in half widthways, with right sides together, lining up the side seams. Pin along this joined-up edge. Starting at the interfacing side, sew a straight line 1cm from the fabric edge. On the jute side, about 5cm from the middle seam, leave a gap of about 13cm (fig C): this is for turning out, so make sure you can get your hand inside! Back stitch a few times at the edges.

10. Along the sewn seams, trim off the excess interfacing close to, but being careful not to nick, the stitching; then clip the corners diagonally (fig D). Press the seams open, wiggling the tip of the iron between the layers of the seam allowance and along the gap.

11. Here's the fun part – creating the boxed bottom. With the seam on one side, find the middle of the bottom section (this is the interfacing end) and hold in place with two vertical pins (fig E).

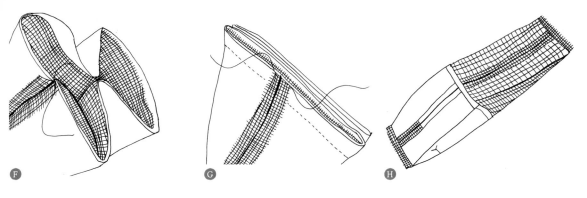

F

G

H

12. Open up the space either side of the pins to make a figure of eight (fig F); then squash flat, bringing the sides (and the seam on one edge) to the pinned centre. Make sure all the folds line up on either side; then pin.

13. Sew across all the fabric with a 1.5cm seam (fig G); double stitch for added strength. (This will be very thick with all the layers, so it's really important to use a good strong needle in your machine.)

15. Repeat steps 11-13 at the jute end (fig H). Then remove the vertical pins (now hidden in the folds) and carefully cut away the excess interfacing.

16. Turn out to the right side, using the gap to pull the fabric through. With your hand inside, push out the corners on both ends (fig I).

17. At this point, push the lining inside the bucket. Part of the jute lining will stay on the outside edge as a neat trim at the top. Make sure the top edge lines up with the top of the patterned fabric section, and press.

18. Topstitch around the jute trim at the top, 2mm from the join with the patterned fabric (fig J).

19. Sew up the inner gap by hand or machine, and add a fancy label if you like.

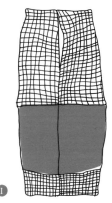

I

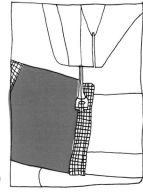

J

Helen Rawlinson is printer and stitcher of many a lampshade. Her simple, timeless prints can also be found covering cushions and tea towels, stuff for kids or whatever else takes her fancy. A Yorkshire lass now living in north-east London with her partner and little boy, Helen's studio is in a converted chocolate factory, where she prints to her heart's content and hammers away on her vintage Bernina sewing machine. *www.helenrawlinson.com*.

Chloé Burrow's
Finger Mouse and Finger Fox

Knit up a friendly family of finger puppets.

Tools

~ set of 2.5mm-3.5mm double-pointed knitting needles
~ yarn needle

Knit skills

~ cast on
~ knit stitch
~ knitting in the round on four needles
~ decreasing: knit 2 together
~ cast off
~ increasing – for the fox only

Materials

~ 4-ply sock yarn in a mousey or fox-like shade
~ 4-ply sock yarn in cream – for the fox only
~ three wooden beads – one dark brown for nose; two light brown for eyes – for each finger puppet

What to do

Finger mouse

1. Cast on 24 stitches using the long-tail method, making sure to end up with a tail of at least 15cm, which forms the tail of the mouse.
2. Divide the stitches evenly between three needles (eight stitches on each needle), making sure this first round is not twisted. Begin knitting stocking stitch in the round (knit every stitch) until you have a tube measuring 7cm in length. Stopping knitting at the end of the round – above where the tail is.
3. Work the next rounds in the following way, decreasing stitches to create a tapered, pointy nose:
   Rnd 1: *k2tog, k to end of needle; rep from * twice more (on the second and third needles).
   Rnds 2-3: k to end.
   Rnd 4: *k2tog, k to the end of the needle; rep from * twice more (on the second and third needles).
   Rnd 5: k to end.
4. Repeat rows 4 and 5 – one decrease round followed by one knit round – until you have three stitches remaining.
5. Cut the yarn leaving a 25cm tail, and thread this onto the yarn needle. Thread the needle through the remaining three stitches; then remove the knitting needles, pull the yarn tight and secure with a couple of stitches.
6. Thread a brown bead on to the yarn and push it against the tip of the nose. Insert your index finger into the knitted tube so that the tail hangs down the back of your hand (fig A).

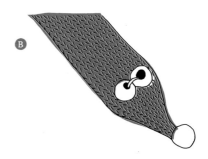

7. Now, looking at the pointed end and the brown bead, push the needle into the bottom of the tip, underneath the bead, and make a small stitch to secure.
8. Now for the eyes. Pass the needle through the inside of the tip to a spot roughly 2cm from the nose, slightly to one side. Feed on the two light brown beads and pass the needle back into the tip of the tube (fig B) – or you can sew on each bead separately, bringing the needle from front to back, for a slightly different look (fig C). Bring the needle up out of the tube and into it again a couple of times, without going through the beads, to secure; then thread the yarn along the bridge of the nose, on the inside. Work the needle in and out of the tip of the nose and finally snip off the excess yarn.

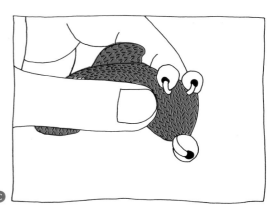

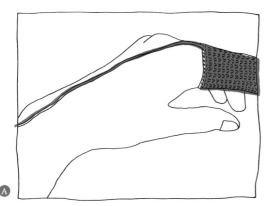

Finger fox

1. Make a finger mouse, completing all steps 1-8.
2. To make the fox tail, cast on nine stitches using the long-tail method and leaving a tail of about 25cm for attaching to the body later.
3. Divide the stitches evenly between three needles (three stitches on each needle) and join in the round, making sure this first round is not twisted.
4. Work the pattern as follows:
   Rnds 1-7: k to end.
   Rnds 8-11: *m1, k to end of needle; rep from * twice more (on the second and third needles).
   You will now have 21 stiches in total.
   Rnds 12-17: k to end.
   Rnd 18: introduce the white yarn, k to end.
   Rnds 19-21: k to end.
   Rnds 22-27: *k2tog, k to end of needle; rep from * twice more (on the second and third needles).
   You will end up with three stitches in total.
5. Cut the yarn leaving a 25cm tail, and thread this into the yarn needle. Thread the needle through the remaining three stitches; then remove the knitting needles, pull the yarn tight and secure with a couple of stitches at the tip. Pull the yarn into the inside of the tail.
6. Stuff the tail with scraps of yarn to pad it out.
7. Thread the strand of yarn at the base of the tail onto a yarn needle and stitch it to the bottom of the body, so that the tail stands up against the back of the fox. Secure the yarn on the inside of the body with a couple of extra stitches, and cut off the excess.

Chloé Burrow learnt to knit aged eight and rediscovered the craft at art school. Despite her course being in Fashion Promotion, she managed to turn her final work into a massive excuse to knit, resulting in knitted versions of designer It Bags. Nowadays, when she isn't indulging her other great passion for swing dancing, Chloé continues to knit and stitch all manner of kitsch, cute and chic things as one half of The Merry Bobbins craft blog. *www.themerrybobbins.co.uk.*

Lou Clarke's **Christmas Pudding Cape**

This seasonal shoulder decoration is proper tasty!

Tools

~ dressmakers' pins
~ scissors
~ set of compasses
~ metre-long ruler
~ iron
~ sewing machine,
    or sewing needle

Materials

~ 70cm x 70cm piece of pattern
    paper or large piece of paper
~ 2m of cotton fabric
~ 1.5m of approx 1cm-wide ribbon
~ sewing thread in the same
    colour as fabric

What to do

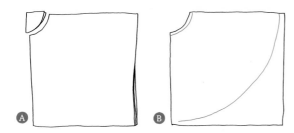

1. Begin with a square of paper measuring 70cm x 70cm and fold in half, then in half again – you have a square a quarter of the size of your original square.
2. Find the corner that has no open edges. Mark out several points that are 6cm from this main corner, and join together to create a curved line (you can use a set of compasses). Cut this corner out (fig A). When opened out, this will make the hole for your head to go through. (This cape fastens with a ribbon to allow for size variation and fits most necks, if you have a very thin or wide neck, however, you can alter this measurement. For a snug fit, measure the circumference of your neck and divide by 6.28 to work out the radius. Use this number to mark out the curve. The actual neck hole will be comfortably 1cm bigger all around, as the pattern includes a 1cm seam allowance.)
3. From the edge of the cut-out curve, measure 28cm all the way round, and cut along this curve (fig B).
4. Unfold to reveal a circular shape with a neck hole in the centre. Cut down one of the folded lines to give you an opening to the cape.
5. Measure 9cm from the neckline at several points, and join to draw out a circle (fig C). This is a guideline for the drip shapes.

6. Now's the fun part where you get to go freestyle with your drip drawing! Starting the drips from the circle you have just drawn, make shapes of varying lengths (fig D). Take into consideration that you will need 1cm seam allowance around all the edges and draw the drips slightly larger than you want them to look on the final cape. Cut out your final shape.

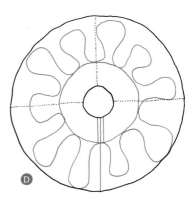

7. Fold the fabric in half, so that the right sides are facing. Pin the cape pattern onto the fabric 1cm from two edges (you still need some fabric left to make a collar) and cut around next to the pattern.
8. Remove the pins and pattern, so you are left with you two matching fabric pieces on top of each other. Pin together at this point, making sure the edges all line up. Sew around all the drips 1cm from the fabric edge on a sewing machine – or you can hand sew it with a running stitch – leaving the neck line open. If you have a free machine embroidery foot for your machine, use this to make the curved lines smoother.

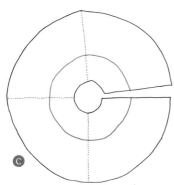

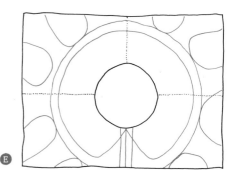

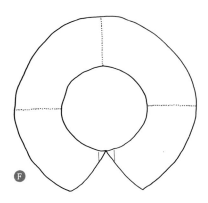

(F)

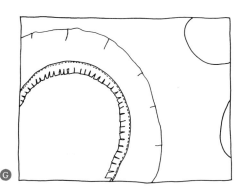

(G)

12. Remove the pattern, and pin the two shapes together on top of one another. Sew around the outside, 1cm from the fabric edge, again leaving the neckline open. Turn right side out to hide the seams and iron.

13. Lay the collar on top of the cape, matching the necklines together, and pin. Sew around the neckline 1cm from the fabric edge. Snip into the seam allowance at 1cm intervals, taking care not to cut into the stitches (fig G).

14. Turn the collar back on itself, folding it over to the other side of the cape, so you are hiding the seams. Iron flat.

15. Cut the ribbon in half. Measure 4cm from the end of one ribbon strip and simply sew this 4cm section underneath the collar at the cape opening (fig H). Repeat this on the other side: you're a Christmas pudding!

9. Snip small V-shapes into the curves of the drips, cutting close to the sewn line but taking care not to cut into the stitches. Turn right side out and iron.

10. Now for the collar. You can cut the collar from your original pattern or trace over if it if you wanted to use your pattern again. Mark 7cm all around neckline. At the opening of the cape draw an upside down V-shape, the centre of the V being at the opening (fig E).

11. Cut out the collar shape (fig F) and pin to doubled-over fabric (right sides together). Cut out next to the pattern to create two pieces exactly the same.

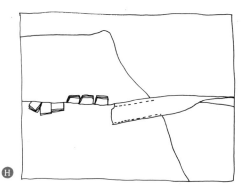

(H)

TIP
You can make the cape in different colours, depending on which cake you fancy being for the evening.

Lou Clarke is a stylist who can be found at the seaside during the week, making toiles and thinking up film and photo-shoot ideas. At the weekends she's in London chatting to customers from behind the counter of the Tatty Devine Brick Lane shop. *www.louclarke.com, loubyswardrobe.blogspot.com.*

Interview with DIYcouture's Rosie Martin

Where do you get your craft inspiration? Human hands are a big inspiration to me - I love the things we do with our hands whether it is building airplanes or making sandwiches. Our hands make our ideas - practical ones and wild ones - into something real. Sometimes we can become frustrated if we don't know how to use our hands to translate a thought to substance, and I hope the DIYcouture books help with this a little bit.

I've recently started to drop in regularly at the British Museum, which is full of exciting handmade objects and textiles from around the world. And London itself is a source of inspiration to me, in all its colourful chaos. I live in Hackney, which is quite an unpolished borough, and itnever fails to surprise me with its people and buildings. I also call in at the Vogue website every now and then, to check out the catwalk shows. Those designers have limitless resources and the results can be spectacular. Alongside that, I also drop in at the Style Bubble blog; writer Susie Bubble bundles on clothing in a really inspiring, creative way. [www.vogue.com, stylebubble.typepad.com.]

How did DIYcouture come about? The light-bulb flash came when I bought a sewing pattern back in 2007. The pattern was to make a wedding dress for my friend Mai, which was a really big deal, and I opened it up to discover an impenetrable wall of coded language and strange indecipherable diagrams. I was flummoxed - and at that point I was a fairly competent DIY seamstress, so I thought, "If I can't understand this, who can?" I had been making my own clothes for about eight years, but I didn't use patterns. I cobbled things together, and followed some diagrams a friend had drawn for me in coloured biro, showing me how to put trousers together, including a zip.

People would often ask me where I got my clothes and when I told them I made them they'd react along the lines of, "I wish I could do that." I was always adamant that they certainly could do it! I didn't have any special skill and I knew that many sewing projects were actually very simple. I really wanted to be able to show people just how easy it is to put good-looking clothes together, and I thought using pictures would be the way to do it."

What's the best thing you've ever made? I'm really proud of the stuff I've made recently, but I think my greatest idea so far has been the DIYcouture cloak. I was working on a music video for an American electro band; the girl in the band dressed up as a sort of tomboy action-hero policeman and I made her a cloak out of shiny navy blue fabric. I just cut a circle out of fabric and then cut a hole in the middle. Then when I was thinking about my collection, about how I wanted it to be elegant and serious but something you could wear every day, the cloak fitted with this. And now the cloak is a very popular garment, on the catwalk and in everyday life!

Do you have favourite designers?
I look at lots of designers.
There's a brand called Proenza
Schouler that I really like
- I like their fabrics. Their
clothes are sort of tomboyish
and clunky. Prada is always
innovative, a little bit
bonkers, plus their clothes are
ethical. And Ada Zanditon: she's
a British ethical designer who
makes really cool geometric
garments; she uses interesting
shapes and bright colours. I
like bright-coloured things.
I loved Les Heal's Spring/
Summer 2010 collection: bold,
colourful, and comfy. Also Jean
Charles De Castelbajac, whose
designs are a bit bonkers, and
also funny. I love the use
of illustration and text in
his prints.

**What's the worst thing you've
ever made?** When I started
DIYcouture, I wanted to make a
whole collection, so I started
by drawing about 50 things on
paper and then decided to make
them. It was definitely a process
of "I made mistakes so you don't
have to make them", rather than
"I know what I'm doing". I was
trying to see if it was possible
to make things, and often it
wasn't. I made terrible things.
Also, when I was 18, I made
a pair of truly disgusting
trousers. I made a pair of
trousers that I really liked in
royal-blue corduroy with giant
red mesh pockets and beads sewn
onto them. They were probably
also horrible, but I liked them
at the time. And I really wanted
to make another pair, in denim,
but for some reason I bought
silver denim. And I made a lot
of pockets trimmed with magenta
ribbon that had small mirrors
set into it… I don't know what

I was thinking! There's no way
they could have come out looking
nice. It's heartbreaking to
put all that effort in and to
have such a disgusting thing.
I've made loads of horrible
things. I don't usually throw
them out. Sometimes I give
them to charity, but sometimes
I feel bad - I think they're
so horrible I don't want
anyone wearing them. But it's
also really important to make
mistakes; you do learn from
something that goes wrong. Also,
people are often an overly harsh
judge of their own work.

Where do you craft? I'm always
in my bedroom, and recently I've
started to use my boyfriend's
bedroom as well. I'm in by
bedroom because I have nowhere
else to go, and it's really
small, so ideally it would
be much bigger. But I've got
pictures all over the wall,
and I've got all my fabric on
shelves. I usually buy fabric
because I really like it, or
because of an idea in my head,
but often it doesn't work out -
so I've got loads and loads of

fabric, and that is inspiring
because I'll look at it and
think in a flash, "I could do
that," and I have little scraps
of paper that I pin on the
fabric so I don't forget.

**Do you feel part of a craft
movement?** Well, what I do is
quite practical, bolting one
bit of fabric onto another, and
I do it on my own, in my room.
And I don't embroider or knit,
or any of those more sociable
craft things. I'm finding out
about these things now, like
the knitting shop [Prick Your
Finger] in Bethnal Green. I
think it's great; and I'm being
asked to do workshops at lots
of crafty events now too. I
think there's definitely a DIY
publishing movement - with
zine fairs etc - and this now
seems to encompass all sorts of
other DIY movements too: DIY
print, DIY fashion, DIY music.
So I feel part of a global DIY
movement, which has been able to
spread so rapidly because of the
internet - people sharing ideas
and processes for free.

DIYcouture's **Mantle**

By Rosie Martin

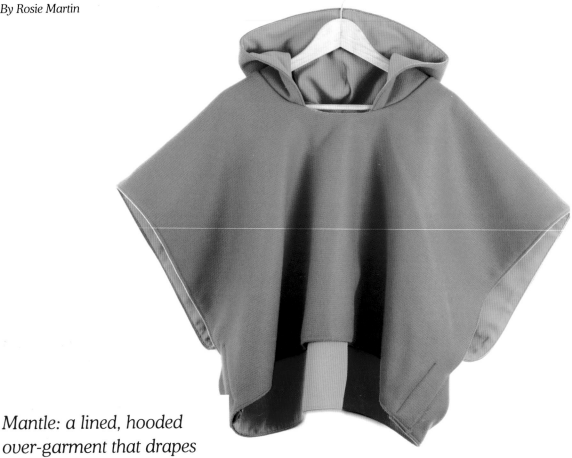

Mantle: a lined, hooded over-garment that drapes over the shoulders, hanging in folds.

Tools

~ dressmakers' pins
~ sewing needle
~ tape measure
~ tailors' chalk, or pencil
~ fabric scissors
~ string
~ a jumper
~ a garment with a hood
~ iron
~ sewing machine

Materials

~ two kinds of fabric: one for outer layer, one for lining. At the very least, you'll need 1.5m of each, depending on how big you want the mantle to be. See steps 1 and 2 to work this out, and add another 0.5m for the hood. Any kind of fabric will work.
~ sewing thread to match both fabrics

What to do

1. Start by cutting a rectangle of fabric. To work out the width, measure from the crook of your elbow up to your shoulder and write this number down. Now measure straight across your body from one shoulder point to the other. Write this down. Add the two together plus an extra elbow-to-shoulder measurement. So, for example:

   Elbow to shoulder = 25cm

   Shoulder to shoulder = 38cm

   25cm + 38cm + 25cm = 88cm

   This is your width measurement. Measure this distance along the bottom edge of your fabric and put a pin in there.

2. Now decide where you would like the bottom edge of your mantle to hang on your body, and measure upwards from this point to where your shoulder meets your neck. For this version that sits at the waist, the measurement was 56cm. Add an extra 2.5cm to this number (ie. 58.5cm) and measure this distance up the side of your fabric; place a pin there. Measure this distance upwards from your width pin too, and put a pin in there (fig A).

3. Now, cut upwards from the width pin to this last pin – you can use a sheet of newspaper to help you mark and cut a straight line. Take the flap of fabric you have created and fold it upwards so the flap is hinged on your the height pins (fig B).

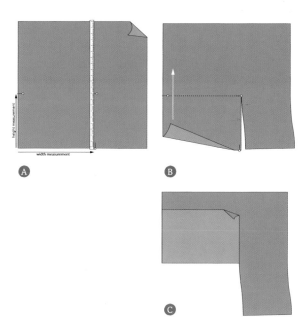

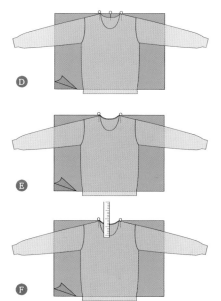

4. Use the folded-over flap as a guide to cut the second half of your piece (fig C); cut around the edges of the flap.

5. This is the main piece of your mantle. You need to cut a hole right in the middle of it so you have somewhere to put your head. With the piece still folded, get a jumper or t-shirt and lay it out so that it sits in the middle of your piece, with the neck at the folded edge of your fabric. Put a pin in the fabric at either side of the neck hole (fig D). Use your tape measure to check that the distance between the neck pin and the edge of your fabric is the same on both sides.

6. Use tailors chalk to draw a scooped line following the curve of the neck edge of your jumper, then cut along this line – you will be cutting through two layers of fabric (fig E).

7. The hole you have made, however, is probably still too small to fit your head. You need to deepen the scoop at the front of the garment. You can measure the depth of the scoop on the front of the jumper (fig F) and measure that distance (11.5cm on this version) down from the centre part of your neck line, and make a short horizontal line in chalk.

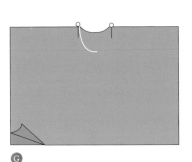

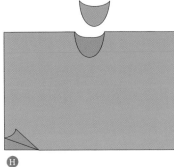

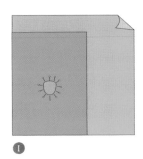

G H I

8. From this line, draw a curve that meets the edge of your neck hole (fig G). Cut along that line.

9. Take the flap you have made and fold it across to the other side of your garment. Use this folded flap as a guide to cut the second half of your neckline exactly the same as the first (fig H). Check that this hole is big enough for your head to fit through.

10. Your outer piece is now ready. You need to cut a lining piece exactly the same. Lay the outer piece out on top of your lining fabric, with the right sides of the fabric facing. Pin the outer piece to the lining fabric around the edge of the hole (fig I). Cut around the edge and cut a matching hole in the lining piece.

11. Now you need to make the hood for your mantle. Firstly, get a piece of string or thread, and cut a length that is the same distance as the distance around the neck edge of your mantle.

12. Get a hoodie (or a coat with a hood) and fold it in half down the centre, so the hood is folded in half vertically. Lay the hoodie on the remainder of the main fabric with the straight front line of the hood

running parallel with the straight vertical edge of your fabric. Draw around the outer curve of the hood. If the garment you are using is made of jersey or stretch fabric and has a snug-fitting hood, draw the hood shape about 10cm taller at the top, so that your hood will fit over your head (fig J).

13. Fold the hood over, marking where is starts on either side; draw a straight horizontal line at both points (fig K). You can now remove your guiding garment. The bottom of your hood needs to form a sort of gentle, stretched S shape. Join your two horizontal lines with a sloping line to mark this shape.

14. The shape you have drawn will form half of your hood. Take the piece of string from step 11 and fold it in half. Lay it out so that it runs along the stretched S at the bottom of the hood. If the string is longer than the line you have drawn, extend the line at the back so that it is the same length as your folded string (fig L).

15. Cut out the first hood piece, then flip it over and use it as a template to cut a mirror image of it from the main fabric (fig M). Then use your first piece as a template to cut two pieces from your lining fabric. Make sure you cut two pieces that mirror each other, rather than two identical pieces, by flipping the template over.

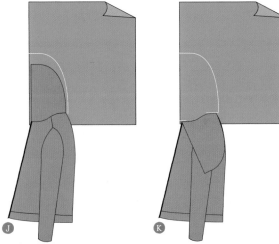

J K

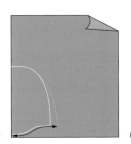

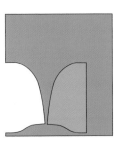

L M

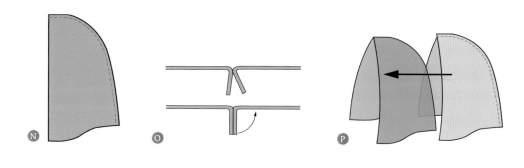

"The mantle can be made with thick fabric for a cosy winter warmer, or thinner fabric for a light springtime top layer."

16. Next, you need to join the hood pieces together in pairs. Lay one of the outer pieces out flat with the right side of the fabric facing upwards towards you; then lay the other piece face down on top of it. Pin all the way along the long curved edge that will form the 'backbone' of your hood. Sew along this line with a straight stitch 1cm from the fabric edge (fig N). Repeat this with the lining pieces.

17. Turn the hood the right way round so that you are looking at the neat edge of your seam. You need to push the flaps of your seam to one side (fig O) and sew them flat, to make a nice neat join. With the right side of your hood facing upwards towards you, sew a line of straight stitch close to the seam (about 1mm-2mm away). Your stitches should catch the flap of fabric on the inside of your hood (the side you can't see) to flatten the seam and neaten the hood. Repeat steps 16-17 with the lining pieces.

18. Now you need to join the lining and outer hood pieces. Turn the lining so that you are looking at the wrong side of the fabric. With the right side of the outer hood piece facing you, insert it inside the lining, so that the right sides of both pieces are touching each other on the inside of the sandwich (fig P).

19. Pin the two together, starting at the central seam and lining the two seams up. Continue pinning all along this raw edge at the front of your hood (fig Q). Sew the pieces together with a straight stitch 1cm from the fabric edge.

20. Then put your hand into the hood-pocket you have formed, and drag the right side of the fabric out, so that you can see the neat seams at the front and the rough edges are hidden inside.

21. Iron the sewn edge of your hood so that the lining and outer fabric sit neatly together, then sew a straight line 1mm-2mm around this edge. It is best to do this with the lining fabric facing upwards towards you so that you can make sure it is not hanging over the outer fabric. The bobbin thread will show on the outside of your hood, so make sure it matches your outer fabric. Sew along the bottom edge of the hood, just in from the rough edges (fig R), to keep the outer and lining fabrics together. Now you have a hood – which you need to attach to your garment…

22. Use your tape measure to find the centre back of the neck hole on the main mantle, and mark it on the outer fabric with a pin.

23. Push the hood into the garment at the neck hole, sandwiching it between the lining and outer fabric, with the outer fabric of the hood brushing against the outer fabric of the mantle and the hood lining against the lining fabric. Take the central seam of your hood and position it exactly where the central pin sits, at the back of the neck edge (fig S). Remove this pin then push it in again so that it goes through the outer fabric, the full hood, and the lining fabric.

24. You need to pin the bottom edge of your hood all the way around the edge of your neck hole. Take it slowly, lining up a few centimetres of the edge of the hood with the neck hole and pinning it (fig T), then dragging the hood round a few centimetres more, lining it up and pinning it. Drag, arrange and pin one full side of your hood into place, then move onto the other side.

25. By the time you have done this (fig U), your mantle will be all rumpled and a bit twisted. Don't worry. The bit you need to concentrate on is the neck line. Hand-stitch the hood into place, through all layers again, making sure you don't have any folds or wrinkles at the neck edge.

26. Now you can sew 1cm around this edge with a straight stitch on your machine. Again, take it slowly, leaving your needle in the down position – poking into your fabric – then lifting the machine foot and turning your fabric slightly before continuing to sew, so that you are following the curve of the neckline (fig V).

27. Trim the fabric at the neck edge so that there is only about 3mm-4mm of fabric sitting outside of the stitching. Sew over this edge with a zigzag stitch.

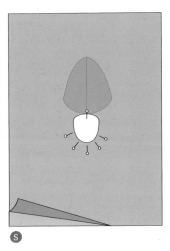

S

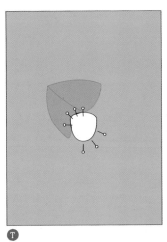

T

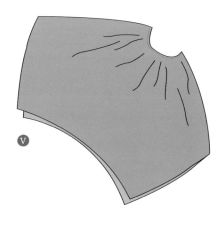

V

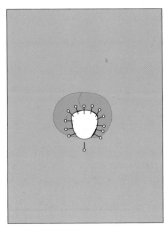

U

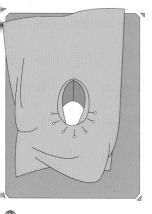
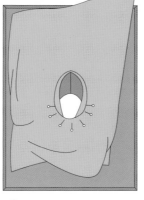

Ⓦ   Ⓧ   Ⓨ   Ⓩ

28. Now turn the garment the right way round (just drag the lining through the neck hole), and lay it out with the lining on top of the outer fabric. If you are using a thick fabric, such as the turquoise fabric used here, it will help to trim the corners diagonally now (fig W), so that you don't end up with lots of layers of folded fabric, which your machine might find difficult to handle. For a thinner fabric, such as cotton, you don't need to do this.

29. Move the lining fabric out of the way so you can concentrate on your outer fabric. You are looking at the wrong side of the outer fabric. You need to hem all four of the straight edges. Fold the edges inwards by about 1cm-2cm, iron them down and sew them into place with straight stitch, close to the edge (fig X).

30. Now you need to hem your lining edges too. Spread the lining fabric on top of the outer fabric (it might help to stick a few pins around the neck edge to make sure the lining fabric is sitting flat). You can again trim the corners.

31. You are looking at the right side of your lining fabric, so you need to fold your hems under, rather than over. Use the outer fabric as a guide to fold the

correct amount of lining fabric under – it should sit 1mm-2mm in from the outer fabric. Iron the folded fabric as you go along each edge, pressing the hem into place.

32. Pin the lining to the outer fabric and sew the two together with a line of straight stitch running close to the edge all the way around (fig Y). Sew with the lining facing upwards towards you, so that you can check it is sitting within the outer fabric. Again, make sure the bobbin thread is the same colour as your outer fabric.

33. Now fold the garment in half so that the bottom, horizontal edges are aligned and overlap the vertical edges at each side by about 4cm (fig Z). Pin the edges together and stitch up from bottom with two rows of straight stitch. You have made a mantle.

TIP
You can also choose to leave your mantle sides unsewn, leaving out step 33 and forming more of a poncho.

Rosie Martin lives in London where she enjoys roaming the streets on her bicycle looking for fabric shops. She has a natural empathy with people who discard an instruction manual in favour of diving straight in, and after years of insisting that making stylish clothes is not that difficult, she invented DIYcouture, providing a picture-based alternative to sewing patterns. In her spare time Rosie plays the drums in noisy psych punk band, BAANEEX, with a range of catchy songs mostly about Dracula. *www.diy-couture.co.uk. www.baaneex.com.*

Tubular Belles

By Victoria Woodcock

Two chunky, fast-to-knit takes on the snood – and a lesson in circular construction!

Soft n' Mossy: knit and purl in the round (the beige one)

Tools

~ 12mm, 70cm circular needle
~ yarn needle
~ stitch marker, or you can use a different coloured piece of yarn

Gauge

~ about 8 stitches and 12 rows over 10cm x 10cm

Materials

~ two 100g balls of chunky yarn (this one uses Rowan Big Wool)

Knit skills

~ cast on
~ knit and purl
~ knitting in the round on a circular needle
~ cast off

Garter Star: beginner knit with a join (the yellow one)

Tools
~ pair of 12mm needles
~ yarn needle

Gauge
~ about 8 stitches and 12 rows over 10cm x 10cm

Materials
~ three or four 50g balls of chunky yarn (this one uses Tait & Style yarn from Prick Your Finger, or you can use Rowan Big Wool)

Knit skills
~ cast on
~ knit
~ slip stitch
~ cast off

TIP
Keep counting that you have the same number of stitches to avoid holes.

What to do

1. With the circular needle, cast on 70 stitches.
2. Join the ends, making sure this first round is not twisted, and place a marker before you start the pattern. This marks the beginning of the round. You will knit the circular snood in one continuous piece; round and round.
3. Start working in a double-moss-stitch pattern as follows:
   Rnd 1: k1, p1 to end.
   Rnd 2: as rnd 1.
   Rnd 3: p1, k1 to end.
   Rnd 4: as rnd 3.
4. Repeat these four rounds until you are nearly out of yarn; you need about 2.5m remaining to cast off. It should measure about 35cm from the cast-on edge.
5. Cast off, keeping to the k1, p1 pattern, and not too tightly, or the shape with gather in at the end.
6. Weave in the loose ends.

What to do

1. Cast on 26 stitches.
2. Knit, knit and knit for a garter stitch pattern. This is basically your all-time classic beginner knit – no purling required. To keep the edges neat, from the second row on, slip the first stitch of each row without knitting it. So the pattern for all rows is: sl1, k to end.
3. Knit until you have nearly no yarn left: you need about 2.5m remaining. It should measure about 70cm-long using three 50g balls. Cast off.
4. Weave in the loose ends of yarn except the long yarn tail at the end. Thread the yarn into the needle, and join the cast-on and the cast-off edges together with a backstitch (or if you're feeling adventurous, look up on the internet about fake grafting). Weave in the end of this yarn.

OUi's **Soy Candle**

By Angela Hodgkinson

A craft that feels a bit like a science experiment but yields a sensual, scented result.

Tools

~ heat-resistant spatula

~ scissors

~ measuring cup/tablespoon

~ scales

~ digital or sugar thermometer

~ old tea towel

~ a kitchen funnel can be useful to help pour the wax

~ double-boiler (which is really just two pots, one of which fits inside the other so that the wax melts over water and not direct flame)

Materials

~ three/four wicks such as natural, lead-free, wax-coated wicks with metal tabs. Or you can coat your own wicks by dipping them into hot wax and allowing to cool

~ 450g soy wax chips – one of the great things about soy wax is it can be easily cleaned up with warm soap and water

~ three/four small to medium glass jars – you can use leftover food jars, just make sure they are clean and dry

~ 2tbsp/30ml non-toxic fragrance oil and/or essential oils, such as cedarwood, rosemary and vanilla

What to do

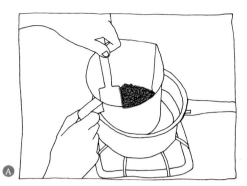

(A)

TIP
To smooth the tops of your candles for a professional finish, you can use a hairdryer on a low heat to slightly melt the tops.

8. When the wax reaches 60°C, add the fragrance oil. Stir gently and continuously for two minutes.
9. Leave the wax to cool to 52°C. Stir once, then slowly pour the wax into the jars. You can centre and straighten the wicks by gently pulling them into place. Allow the wax to cool and harden overnight.
10. Once the wax is completely hardened (12-24 hours), remove the pegs and trim the wicks to 0.5cm. You can decorate the jars and their lids with ribbon, tags, fabric etc.

1. Place the wicks alongside the sides of the jars and trim them so they stand 3cm-4cm above the jar opening.
2. Fill the bottom pot of the double boiler with about 6cm-7cm of water and bring to boil.
3. As the water is heating up, measure out 450g of wax chips and place them in the second pot. Measure out the fragrance oil, keeping it separate from the wax.
4. When the water boils, turn it down to a slight simmer. Add the pot of wax to water, stirring occasionally with the spatula as the wax melts (fig A). Soy wax will melt at around 45-55°C, although you will be heating the wax to 75-85°C.
5. While the wax melts, dip the wick tabs into the semi-melted wax and use this to glue the tabs to the centre of the jar bottoms (fig B).
6. Thread the top of the wick into the hinge of a clothes peg – it will keep the wick secure and centred during pouring. Rest the peg on the top of the jar and pull the wick up straight (fig C).
7. Heat the wax to 75-85°C. Remove from the heat and place the pot on top of a folded over tea towel. Leave the wax to stand and cool to 60°C, stirring occasionally.

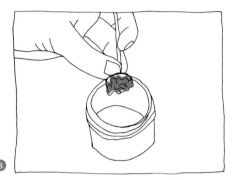

(B)

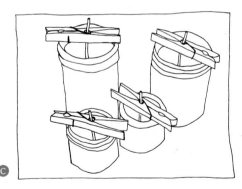

(C)

Angela Hodgkinson bounces back and forth between Brooklyn and her home state of Oklahoma, incorporating the values and aesthetics of both places into her work. She believes in using safe and healthy, natural materials to make thoughtful, eco-conscious and modern products for the artful home. *www.bonjourOUi.bigcartel.com, www.various-projects. blogspot.com.*

Clutch Me's **Clutch Bag**

By Jess Fawcett

An easy-to-sew number just big enough to carry all your essentials.

Tools

- ~ dressmakers' pins
- ~ sewing needle
- ~ stitch ripper
- ~ scissors
- ~ knitting needle, or other poking implement
- ~ iron
- ~ sewing machine (optional)

Materials

- ~ 30cm x 40cm piece of cotton fabric for the outside
- ~ 30cm x 40cm piece of cotton material for the lining
- ~ two 30cm x 40cm pieces and two 3cm x 3cm pieces of extra-heavy iron-on interfacing
- ~ magnetic snap fastener
- ~ sewing thread to match the outside fabric

What to do

1. Cut out the pieces of fabric. Lay out the lining fabric so that the wrong side is facing upwards. Place the interfacing on top, with the fusible side facing down. Applying steady pressure, use a hot iron and plenty of steam to bond the interfacing to the fabric. Repeat with the outer fabric.
2. Align the outer and lining pieces, with the right sides together. Pin along three sides (the two longer edges and one short one), with the pins at right angles to the fabric edge (fig A).

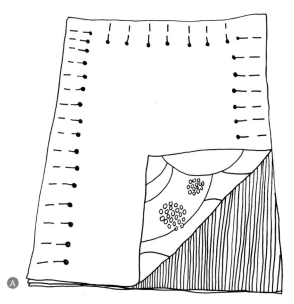

3. Using the sewing machine and a straight stitch, or a hand sewn running stitch, sew along the three pinned edges about 1cm from the fabric edge. You should be able to safely sew over the pins, but be careful.
4. Remove the pins, and snip off the corners diagonally close to but not cutting through the stitches.
5. Turn the whole thing right side out, using a knitting needle or the end of a blunt pair of scissors to poke the corners out. Press flat.

6. Fold the bag into three sections, rather like an envelope. Make the first fold about 13cm from the unsewn edge, and the second about 12cm from the sewn edge to form the top flap. Iron to hold the folds in place.

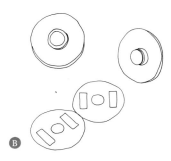

7. Now for the magnetic fastener. This has two halves, and each half has a washer (a flat disc with two rectangular slots) that goes at the back of the fabric as well as the magnetic part (fig B).
8. The first half of the fastener, with the bit that sticks out, should be fixed on the inside of the top edge of the bag. Find the centre point of the top (sewn) side and place a washer about 3.5cm in from the edge of the bag, on the lining, so that the rectangular slits are vertical (fig C).
9. Mark the position of the two rectangular holes with a pencil; then use the stitch ripper to carefully pierce just the lining fabric (not the outside layer) along the pencil lines.
10. Trace the holes of the clasp washer onto one of the 3cm x 3cm pieces of interfacing, and pierce the holes in the same way.

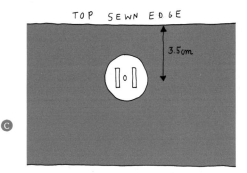

11. Push the prongs of the front half of the snap fastener through the holes in the lining fabric. Now you want to push the prongs through the interfacing and the washer, on the inside of the bag, which is a little tricky. Line up the holes in the interfacing and the washer, and hold with the interfacing facing up. Unfold the bag and reach up inside to where the prongs are; push the prongs through the interfacing and into the washer (fig D). Ease the prongs downwards and outwards until flat.

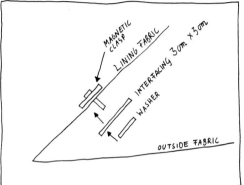

"You can use any fabric for your bag. I like to use heavier, vintage materials – old curtains are ideal!"

14. Fold over to bring the fastener together, and iron so that all the edges are neatly lined up. Unfasten, and fold the flap up. Pin the two layers together at either side (fig E). Sew up the sides about 1cm from the fabric edge, using a straight stitch on your machine or a running stitch if you are hand sewing (the fabric will be tough to get through here as there are lots of layers, so use a thimble to save your fingers), sewing backwards at both ends to add strength.

12. Refold the bag and mark where the magnetic fastener touches the outside fabric. Position the other washer here and follow steps 9-12 to attach the other half of the magnetic clasp, this time cutting just through the outer fabric.

13. Now you can sew up the open edge above the second half of the clasp. Fold the rough edges of the fabric inwards to form a neat straight edge; iron and pin in place. You can either sew across the top with a straight stitch on a sewing machine (make sure your pins are at right-angles if you do this) or you can hand-sew the two fabrics together using small, neat whipstitches (or look up on the internet how to sew a slipstitch – although time consuming, the stitches are almost invisible).

Jess Fawcett began making bags for her nearest and dearest while living in Tokyo several years ago – and many of her designs are crafted from her stash of Japanese fabrics acquired during this time. Now residing in London, she makes bags and knits stuff under the name Clutch Me. *www.clutch-me.co.uk.*

Legwarmers for Little Ones

By Victoria Woodcock

Master knitting on four needles with simple stripes for fashionable kids.

What to do

Tools

~ set of 5mm double-pointed needles
~ stitch marker
~ yarn needle

Materials

~ aran-weight yarn in two different colours (yarn A and B), such as Rowan Pure Wool Aran

Knit skills

~ cast on
~ knit and purl
~ knitting in the round on four needles
~ cast off

Gauge

~ 20 stitches and 26 rows over 10cm x 10cm

Measurements

To fit:	1-2yrs	2-3yrs	3-4yrs
Calf circumference:	17cm	19cm	21cm

1. Cast on 32 (36; 40) stitches in yarn A.
2. Divide the stitches onto three needles so that there are an even number of stitches on each (10, 10 and 12, for example).
3. Join the ends, making sure this first round is not twisted, and place a marker before you start knitting. This marks the beginning of the round. You will knit the legwarmers in one continuous piece; round and round.
4. Work in the round as follows:
   Rnds 1-8: k1, p1 to end.
   Rnds 9-16: knit every stitch.
   Rnd 17: join in B. Knit.
   Rnds 18-32: knit.
   Rnd 33: join in A. Knit.
   Rnds 34-48: knit.
   Rnd 49: join in B. Knit.
   Rnds 50-56: knit.
   Rnds 57-64: k1, p1 to end.
5. Cast off, keeping to the k1, p1 pattern, and not too tightly, so as to keep some stretch at the end.
6. Turn inside out, and weave in the loose ends.

Andrea Garland's
Fabulously Thrifty Body Oil

A fragrant, moisturising mixture to make body oil, body polish and honey bath milk.

Materials

For the Fabulously Thrifty Body Oil
~ 100ml of sweet almond oil, or another base oil such as coconut or sesame seed. Don't use baby oil, though, as it's petroleum based and clogs up pores
~ 16 drops of mandarin essential oil
~ 10 drops of geranium essential oil
~ a glass bottle or jar

For the body polish
~ 30ml of Fabulously Thrifty Body Oil
~ 60g of Epsom salts (available from Boots or on Amazon. You could also use table salt or sugar, but avoid sea salt as this is too coarse for the skin)

For the honey bath milk
~ 20ml of Fabulously Thrifty Body Oil
~ 60ml of full-fat milk (it must be full fat for the oil and honey to mix in well)
~ a teaspoon of honey

For the packaging
~ a piece of cotton fabric big enough to cover the bottle or jar – if it's vintage, even better
~ rickrack braid
~ all-purpose glue

Tools
~ glass beaker or measuring jug
~ metal spoon and fork
~ scissors or pinking shears

What to do

Body oil

1. Pour 100ml of sweet almond oil into a glass beaker. Add the essential oils and stir.
2. Pour the mixture into a glass jar or bottle.
3. Massage oil onto your body as a moisturiser or to treat dry-skin areas.

For the scrub

1. Measure 60g of salt or sugar into a bowl.
2. Pour in 30ml of Fabulously Thrifty Body Oil and stir thoroughly.
3. In a warm bath, massage the scrub onto your skin taking care to avoid sensitive areas and your face.

For the bath milk – use on day of making!

1. Pour 60ml of full-fat milk into a bowl.
2. Add 30ml of Fabulously Thrifty Body Oil.
3. Add a teaspoon of honey
4. Wisk with a fork until all the ingredients have blended together.
5. Pour into a warm bath; lie back and relax.

Packaging

1. Measure out a piece of vintage fabric that will fit around the straight sides of the jar or bottle (fig A).
2. Cut out, with pinking shears if you have them.
3. Glue edges of fabric with adhesive and carefully stick to straight sides of bottle, pulling the edges tight so there is no give once stuck
4. Glue rickrack over the fabric edges.

A

TIP
Experiment with other essential oils to find the fragrance that suits you best.

Andrea lives in east London in a house packed full of treasures from car-boot sales, auctions, junk shops and even skips. Her love of vintage has become intermingled with her love of natural skincare lotions and potions, and she fills antique tins, pillboxes and compacts with soothing balms for the lips, face and body. When she isn't mixing and making in her kitchen, she likes to sing in a folk band, jog with her dog and speak French. *www.andreagarland.co.uk*.

Kristie Maslow's
Children's Pillowcase Dress

Grandma's linen closet is the perfect starting point for a sweet summer dress...

Tools

~ dressmakers' pins
~ safety pin
~ tape measure
~ tailors' chalk, or a pencil
~ iron
~ pinking shears (optional)
~ sewing machine (optional)

Materials

~ pillowcase
~ approx 30cm of 0.5cm-wide elastic
~ 2m of bias binding
~ sewing thread to match pillowcase and bias binding

What to do

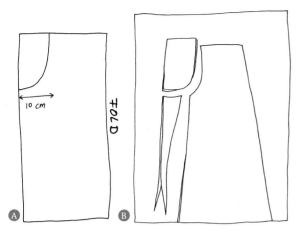

10 cm

± 70 cm

A

B

5. Unfold the pillowcase and turn inside out. Line up the edges and pin. Sew along the diagonal side seams of the dress with a straight stitch, or a running stitch if you are working by hand, 1cm from the fabric edge. To prevent fraying, you can cut along the seam allowance with pinking shears if you have them, or sew along the edges with a zigzag stitch.

1. Measure your little girl from her armpit to about the knee (or where you want the dress hem to rest).

2. Fold the pillowcase in half lengthways, and measure this distance up the side opposite the folded edge, from the bottom (open edge). From this point, draw a J-shaped curve that extends about 10cm into the fabric horizontally then continues up to the top (closed) edge vertically (fig A). This will be the armhole.

3. Mark out a point about 5cm along the horizontal line of the J shape. From this point, draw a straight diagonal line to the corner of the hem (the open end of pillowcase). Cut along this line (fig B). This tapers the dress at the sides so it's not too boxy.

4. Measure 10cm up from the horizontal segment of the "J" towards the top edge of the pillowcase. Draw a horizontal line at this point and cut along it (fig C).

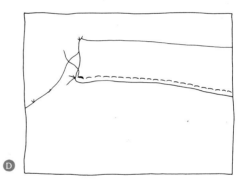

D

6. Along the top edge, fold over 0.5cm of fabric on both sides of the pillowcase; then press flat with an iron. Fold over another 1cm to hide the rough edge, and press again. Sew along the folds, 2mm from the edge, and leaving the ends open (fig D).

7. Cut the elastic into two 15cm lengths. Attach a safety pin to one piece, and thread it through one of the channels you have just created until it emerges at other end. Pin both ends of the elastic to the fabric, and repeat on the other side with the second piece of elastic.

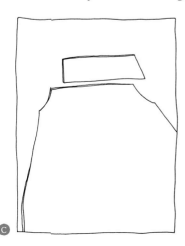

C

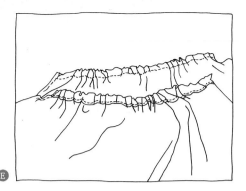

E

11. The extra lengths of the bias binding become the straps. Tuck in the raw ends of bias tape at the ends of the straps. Starting at one end, position the short-fold side of the tape facing up, and stitch along the strap close to the fold. Continue over the elastic into the armhole area (fig G). Since the longer folded side is in the back, if you follow the edge along the front, you should be sewing over the bias binding at the back also. Continue all the way to the end of the second strap. Repeat on the other side.

8. Sew the ends of channels shut, catching the elastic in the stitching to secure, so that the fabric is gathered around the elastic (fig E).

9. Cut two pieces of bias binding measuring about 1m each. With the dress inside out, find the centre of the bias binding. Now look at the bias binding tape and you will notice that one folded side is slightly shorter than the other side. Unfold the tape and starting at the centre point of the tape and one of the side seams at the top of the dress, pin the raw edge of the wider side of the tape along the raw edge of armhole, so that the right side of the tape is touching the wrong side of the fabric. Pin from elastic to elastic and sew along the raw edges, 2mm in from the edge. Repeat on the other side.

10. Refold the bias binding tape. When you do so, the line you just stitched becomes covered and disappears. Fold the tape over to the right side of the dress, so that the centre fold of the tape covers the raw edge of the armhole and the short folded side will be on the outside of the dress. Pin in place to secure (fig F).

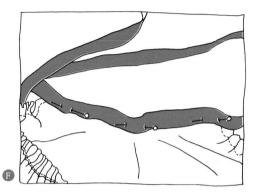

F

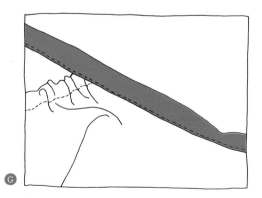

G

Kristie Maslow is a self-taught seamstress and quilter who is constantly scribbling project ideas on napkins and old receipts. She is a mum to three little munchkins, a wife to a patient man who is trained to say, "Wow, you made that?" and a partner in a busy dental practice. She likes comedies, ice cream, days at the beach and knitting in inappropriate places. *www.ocd-obsessivecraftingdisorder.blogspot.com*.

Photograph: greatglasseyephotography.com

Naomi Ryder's **Couched Hummingbird**

Lift a dull cardigan with an embroidered illustration.

Tools

~ dressmakers' pins
~ embroidery needle
~ scissors
~ embroidery hoop (optional)
~ tailors' chalk, pencil, or disappearing felt pen
~ non-stick, greaseproof paper
~ masking tape
~ iron

Materials

~ cardigan, jumper, T-shirt or shirt
~ embroidery thread or fine wools in various shades of blue and green
~ small pieces of silk chiffon, organza or raw silk – here bright pink raw silk is used for the head, and blues and greens for the feathers
~ double-sided iron-on transfer adhesive, such as Bondaweb
~ sewing thread (optional)

What to do

1. Iron your chosen item of clothing and decide on the position and size of the illustration. Photocopy and adjust the size of the hummingbird template on page 239.
2. Trace the line drawing onto the garment. The best way to do this is to tape the photocopy to a window, then tape the garment on top so that you can see the illustration through the fabric. Draw over the image lightly with a tailors' chalk pencil.
3. Now for the couching. Lay the embroidery thread down in a line, following a section of the drawing (fig A). Make sure to leave 5cm-8cm of extra thread at the beginning and end of each line (so you can thread these pieces to the back and secure later).
4. Cut a new length of the same thread, approx 30cm in length. You are basically going to sew over and around the thread you laid out in step 3, trapping it in place with small neat stitches. So, at one end of the thread line, bring the needle from the back to the front of the fabric, and make a couple of small stitches on the spot to secure the thread. Now put the needle into the fabric just the other side of the laid-down thread; and bring it up again about 1cm further along, again switching to the opposite side of the laid-down thread. (fig B). The needle should be back on the side of the thread you started on.

"I absolutely love couching – it is easy to work with but also very effective. You can create an image that is really graphic, as couching can have corners and curves, thick and thin lines."

5. Continue in this way around the section of the design. If you are working on a stretch fabric, such as a cardigan or T-shirt, work in small sections, then tie off the thread (make a few stitches on the spot to secure) and start again, so as to keep the stretch in the garment. You can experiment with the thickness of your lines by splitting up the embroidery strands.
6. Once you've got the hang of the couching technique, think about where you want to add in fabric – as you will want to couch over the top of some of these. Cut out fabric shapes and arrange.

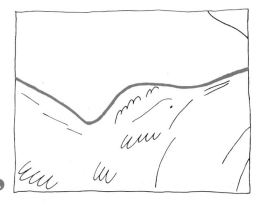

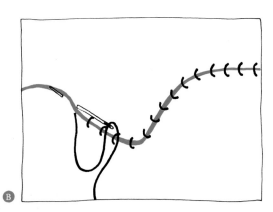

7. To attach the fabric shapes, cut a piece of Bondaweb slightly larger than the fabric. Place a piece of non-stick paper on an ironing board, and place the fabric face down on the paper. Position the Bondaweb on top, paper side up, and iron.

8. Peel off the paper and trim the Bondaweb to the fabric edge (fig C). Place the piece, bonded side down, in the correct position; then cover with the non-stick paper and iron.

9. Bonding does not permanently hold the pieces – it just looks smart and gives you a nice structure to work with – so carry on couching over the top of the fabric to secure (fig D).

10. To make loose feathers, as at the tail of this design, don't attach the fabric shapes with Bondaweb: instead, layer a number of pieces of fabric, pin in place and just couch over the top. You can add little running stitches in sewing thread to hold down certain sections.

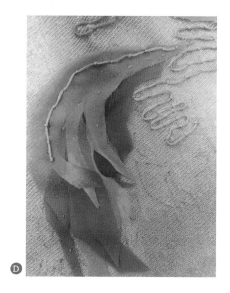

(D)

"I thought about the design a little like a tattoo."

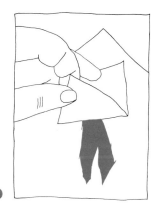

(C)

11. To finish, bring all the loose thread ends to the back and secure by working them in and out of the last stitches with the needle. This will keep the garment nice and flat. Trim ends, and you're done.

Naomi Ryder loves illustrating with stitch. She works from her studio at Cockpit Arts in Deptford, London, and is inspired by the beauty and humour of everyday routines. Her products include cushions, cards, T-shirts, plates and mugs, and she also sells embroidered artwork to commission. Recent commissions include the Southbank Centre, Domino Records and Habitat. Her work has been exhibited at the Queen Elizabeth Hall and Canary Wharf. *www.naomiryder.co.uk.*

Lucie Ellen's **Bunting Necklace**

Capturing the spirit of
fetes, carnivals and make
do and mend!

Tools

~ ruler
~ hacksaw or piercing saw
~ sandpaper
~ hand drill with a 2mm bit
~ clamp
~ small jewellery pliers –
  two pairs are helpful

Materials

~ approx 10cm x 10cm piece
  of plywood or MDF, about
  5mm thick
~ acrylic paint in a range of
  colours
~ acrylic varnish
~ approx 50cm-long jewellery
  chain
~ jewellery clasp
~ eight jewellery jump rings,
  approx 10mm in diameter

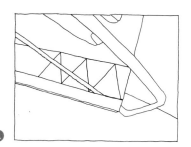

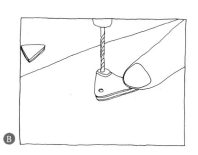

What to do

1. On the wood, mark out five triangles of the same size. These ones are about 2.5cm at their largest point.
2. Clamp the wood to a table and carefully cut out the triangles with the saw (fig A). Don't worry if they are slightly wonky; it adds to the charm, and you will be able to neaten things up with sandpaper.
3. Sand down the edges of each triangle so they are smooth; no ragged bits or sharp points.
4. Paint one side of each triangle with your choice of colours, or patterns – spots, stripes, squiggles – and leave to dry for about an hour.
5. Once dry, neaten up any paint mishaps on the edges by sanding them off, then give each triangle a coat of varnish. Leave to dry again.

6. Now for the holes. Place one triangle on a scrap piece of wood, and clamp into place. Create a hole in the two corners of the shortest side by positioning the drill bit a few millimetres from the edge, keeping it at a right angle and drilling very firmly (fig B). Do this for each triangle.
7. The jump rings are used to link the flags together. Hold the jump ring with the two pair of pliers (one on each side of the small slit) and twist the ring toward you. (You should never pull the ring apart, as you won't be able to get the ends to match up again). Slip two flags onto one ring (fig C), making sure they are facing the same way, then close the jump ring by twisting it as before with the pliers. Do this with four rings between the flags.
8. "Cut" the chain in half by twisting apart one of the links. At each end of the flag garland, open up a jump ring and slip on a flag and a length of chain. Adjust the necklace to your desired length, then attach a clasp to one end, and another jump ring to the other.

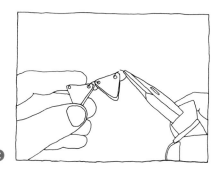

Lucie Ellen runs her accesories and homewares line from her garden shed in a small village in rural Suffolk, England. Using reclaimed wood and vintage china, she creates lovely things to wear and use. When not in the shed, she can be found sewing bizarre items of clothing on her old Singer, making pasta and bread, walking on the shore with her girlfriend, and thinking about where she's going on holiday next. www.lucie-ellen.com, www.etsy.com/shop/lucie0ellen.

Little Glowing Lights' **Garlands**

By Catherine Miller

The perfect preparation for a party occasion.

Dotty Doily Garland

Tools

~ set of compasses
~ large needle to fit the ribbon/thread
~ scissors, or a circle punch or cutter
~ pinking shears
~ small craft hole punch or eyelet tool

Materials

~ paper doilies around 10cm in diameter
~ coloured paper to your liking – those with different textures work well
~ 2m or more of ribbon or thread, approx 5mm wide (or whatever will thread through your needle)

What to do

1. Cut out a number of different-sized circles – about 5cm, 3.5cm and 2.5cm in diameter – from the coloured paper, using a combination of scissors and pinking shears. The number of circles you need will depend on how long you want the garland to be.
2. You need one larger 5cm circle and one of either of the smaller sizes to sit in front of each doily, and one of the smaller sizes for in between the paper doilies.
3. Punch two little holes about 1cm apart close to the edge of the 5cm circles and the smaller circles to be used in between doilies. The small circles to be used on top of the doilies will only need one hole.
4. To make the garland, thread the ribbon into the needle and slip through the two holes on one of the smaller single circles. Slide the circle carefully along the ribbon for the length you would like the garland to be, so that it is at the far end from the needle.
5. Then thread the ribbon from the back into one of the holes on the paper doily that is close to the centre. From here on the pattern will be as follows: thread the ribbon through one hole of the larger-sized circle, followed by the small circle with one hole, back through the second hole of the larger circle and then thread into a second hole in the paper doily so that the garland sits evenly and the ribbon is flat through the layers of paper. Add another single smaller circle, through two holes, and then through the back of the next doily. Repeat the process.

Colourful Felt Garland

Tools
~ scissors
~ sewing needle to fit thread

Materials
~ squares of brightly coloured felt
~ thick sewing thread

What to do

1. Cut out lots of little circles from the felt of approx 2.5cm and 1.5cm diameter. As before, the number of circles you need will depend on how long you want the garland to be.
2. Thread up the needle and sew two small running stitches (in and out of the fabric twice, in a straight line) near to the edge of one felt circle. Slide the circle along the thread for the length you would like the garland to be, so that it is at the far end from the needle.
3. Add more circles, mixing up the sizes and colours, as in step two. As you push the circles along, gather them into colourful little clusters.

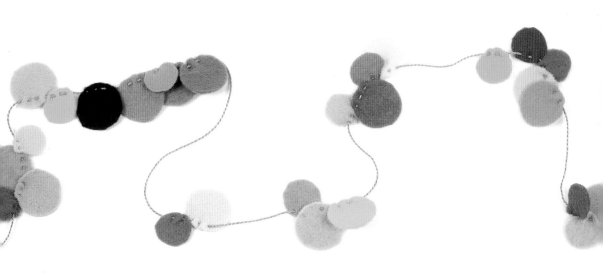

Catherine Miller lives in Hobart, Australia. She is a daydreamer who loves art, craft, music, cooking and taking lots of pictures, which she shares on her blog, Little Glowing Lights. One day she would like a ginger cat and to have a job that is more creative, but right now she is happy making little bits and pieces to display in her flat and occasionally sell in her Etsy store. *www.littleglowinglights.blogspot.com, www.littleglowinglights.etsy.com.*

Aurora Bloom's **Button Rings**

By Raye McKown

The everyday fastener becomes cheap and cheerful hand candy.

Regular buttons

Tools

~ sewing needle
~ sandpaper
~ pliers (if your button has a shank)

Materials

~ buttons
~ adjustable ring base
~ sewing thread
~ strong all-purpose glue

What to do

1. Choose a fancy button from your stash.
2. If your button has a shank (loop at the back), this needs to be removed with a set of pliers. If this leaves little stumps, sand them down flat. Then glue the button to the ring base and leave to dry.
3. For a different look, you can use a large button and sew a smaller button on top before gluing.

Fabric-covered buttons

Tools

~ scissors
~ pliers
~ sewing needle

Materials

~ metal self-cover buttons (29mm ones work well) – these come in two parts, a curved front section and a flat back plate
~ adjustable metal ring base
~ approx 6cm x 6cm piece of thin fabric
~ sewing thread
~ strong all-purpose glue
~ embellishments such as sequins, beads, lace, flat-backed gems etc

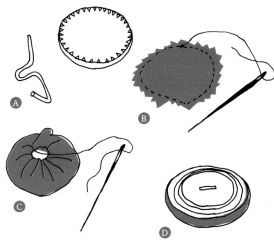

What to do

1. Remove the metal shank (the loop at the back of the button) with a pair of pliers (fig A).
2. Place the front button part (the curved bit) in the middle of the square of material and draw a circle around it, leaving a margin of about 1 cm.
3. If you want to embellish the fabric with any embroidery – your initials, perhaps – do so now inside the centre of the circle.
4. Cut out the fabric circle and, with a needle and thread, sew little running stitches around the circumference of the circle (fig B) – don't tie off or cut the thread yet.
5. Lay the fabric face down and place the curvy part of the button on top of it. Pull the thread to gather the fabric loosely so that it is stretched flat across the curved front of the button (fig C). Don't pull too tight, or it will be difficult to attach the back of the button. Tie the thread and cut.
7. Press the metal backing over the gathered fabric, and click it firmly into place (fig D).
8. Glue the ring base onto the back of the button. You can now stick on any little buttons, sequins or beads you might have in your craft cupboard. Leave to dry.

> **TIP**
> **Why stop at rings?**
> **Glue buttons to brooch backs**
> **or even cuff links.**

Raye McKown sells jewellery, knitted and crocheted accessories and handmade cards in her online shop, Aurora Bloom, and delivers jewellery-making and paper-craft workshops. She lives in Oldham with her husband, Mike, and cat, Lily, and loves nothing better than roaming around car-boot sales and charity shops picking up old lace, buttons and beads to use in her projects. *www.aurorabloom.com, www.etsy.com/shop/RayeBroxapCrafts*.

Interview with Ebony Bizys of Hello Sandwich

What are your earliest crafting memories? I've always loved making things by hand and admired objects handmade by others. My mother started me making crafts at a very young age. Instead of playing with regular toys, my mum and I would line up colourful buttons and ribbons from her fabric shop. My family background is Lithuanian, and in keeping with eastern European traditions I remember that at Easter time we would enjoy hang dyeing and painting boiled eggs.

When did you start up your blog? I started Hello Sandwich about two years ago as a place to record and share the things that inspired me.

Where do you craft? I make craft in my mini-me Shimokitazawa, Tokyo apartment. Sometimes I load my bike basket up with craft materials, call a friend, and head to a table in Yoyogi Park to make craft outdoors. It's so lovely and relaxing. I've also started hosting regular craft workshops in Tokyo, which is great fun. I love crafting with others.

What is the most amazing thing you have ever made? I am most proud of the Hello Sandwich Gift Wrapping Zine. It's a collection of creative gift-wrapping techniques guaranteed to pretty up any present. The projects include a confetti bow and how to make a gift bag from a sheet of paper. A while ago, I had a little clothing label that I would sell at markets and to a few boutiques. Some of the garments I made at that time are my favourite things.

What is your biggest crafting disaster? I must confess, there have been a few 'moments' with my mother's hot glue gun over the years…

What is your dream craft project? I would love to do a window display one day, or make a paper set for a video or photo shoot.

Do you feel part of a craft movement? I hadn't really thought about it, but I'm happy if through Hello Sandwich I am able to inspire others to have a "crafternoon", or just make something by hand.

Hello Sandwich's
Gift Bag, Tag and Confetti Bow

By Ebony Bizys

Add extra paper personality to the perfect present.

Handmade gift bag

Tools
~ ruler
~ scissors

Materials
~ 56cm x 50cm piece of paper or wrapping paper – makes a bag 26cm-high (not including handles)
~ sticky tape, or washi tape
~ sticky-back plastic or masking tape
~ handles from an old paper shopping bag, or two 22cm x 34cm pieces of thin paper or newspaper to make your own

What to do

1. Cut a sheet of paper measuring about 56cm (width) x 50cm (height), and fold the 56cm edge in half.
2. Fold over one of the edges opposite the fold by about 4cm, turning the edge inwards; then press flat. Tuck the other paper edge under this folded edge, so they overlap, and tape together (fig A).
3. Fold up the bottom of the bag by about 5cm, and press down, forming a crease (fig B).

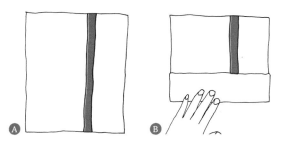

4. Open out one side of the base. Lining up the side crease with the bottom fold, flatten the corners into a triangle shape (fig C). Repeat at the other side of the base.
5. Fold up the bottom edge of the base to meet the fold above it (fig D).
6. Fold the top edge of the base down to the same fold and tape together (fig E).
7. Put your hand inside the bag and push out the base so that it is rectangular and the bag will stand up.

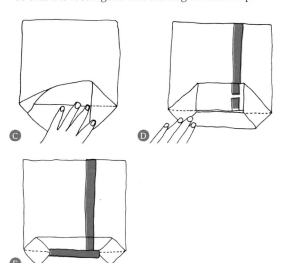

8. Decide on your handles. You can take some off an old paper shopping bag (fig F), or you can make your own from thin paper. To do so, cut the paper to 22cm x 34cm and fold a triangle shape in one corner about 7cm at the height of the triangle; then roll the paper into a stick. Flatten slightly and make an arch in the middle to form a handle. If they are too thick to bend, unroll some of the paper and cut it off.
9. Cut two rectangles of sticky-back plastic (or masking tape) to fit in the top of either side of the bag. Peel the backing off the plastic, and position the handle ends at either side of the rectangle, lining up the ends with the bottom edge of the plastic, and looping the top so it is not twisted.
10. Stick the handles inside the top of the gift bag on either side.

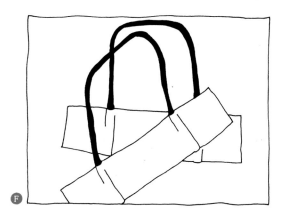

TIP
Do you ever receive envelopes you think are too cute to discard? Use them to make a mini gift bag – just cut open one side, flatten out the bottom and add handles.

Confetti bow

Tools
~ scissors
~ ruler
~ hole punch (optional)

Materials
~ approx 15cm x 20cm of sticky-back plastic for a medium-sized bow
~ confetti, or multicoloured scraps of paper/tissue paper to make your own
~ sticky tape, or ribbon

What to do

1. Cut a rectangle of sticky-back plastic measuring about 15cm x 20cm, depending on the size bow you desire (try 9cm x 12cm to create a smaller bow, or 21cm x 28cm for an XXL version).
2. Peel the backing from the sticky-back plastic and sprinkle one half of the sheet with confetti (fig A). You can make multicoloured dots of your own by hole-punching into different coloured sheets of paper and/or tissue paper.
3. Fold the blank side of sticky-back plastic over on top of the confetti side (fig B), trying to keep the plastic free from dreaded creases – remember when you used to cover your school books in this stuff?
4. At centre point of the longer side of the rectangle, squish the two edges together to form a bow shape, and fasten with sticky tape or a ribbon.

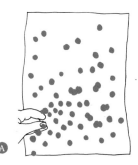

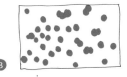

Gift tags

Tools
~ scissors
~ glue stick
~ eyelet punch, or a hole punch

Materials
~ images to collage from magazines, vintage books etc
~ small piece of cardboard
~ approx 15cm-long cord or ribbon
~ small eyelet (optional)

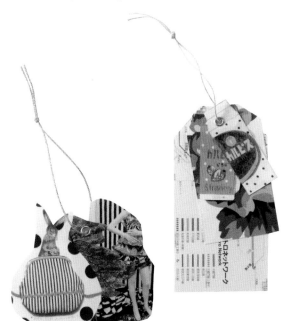

What to do

1. Cut out images and design your tag; then stick the collage elements onto cardboard and cut out. You can make different-sized designs to layer.
2. Make a hole at the top centre of the tags. Using an eyelet punch to add an eyelet will add a professional finish.
3. Tie cord or ribbon through the hole. You could also use a few different threads on one tag.

Ebony Bizys is an Australian graphic designer, artist, crafter and zine-maker who lives in Tokyo, spending her days freelance designing, making zines, learning Japanese and riding her bike around taking photos. Ebony shares her love of all things Japanese on her blog, Hello Sandwich, and recently launched Hello Sandwich Craft TV, with how-to videos and international craft workshops via Skype. She also blogs for *Vogue* Japan and trend reports for British website Stylus. *www.hellosandwich.blogspot.com.*

Hannah Wardle's
Paper-Cut Light Box

*Layers of pattern-cut paper
add texture and intrigue to
a simple light in a box.*

Tools

- sandpaper
- hammer
- craft knife
- metal ruler
- cutting matt or other cutting surface, such as an old sheet of wood
- saw, such as a junior hacksaw
- drill – hand drill or power drill – with 8mm bit
- 2mm or 3mm drill bit (this should be a slightly smaller diameter than the screws for the lamp holder)
- pliers
- Pozidriv/Phillips screwdriver
- small flathead screwdriver – for wiring plug

Materials

- wooden wine box at least 15cm deep – ask at an off license

From DIY store
- plastic lamp holder with fixing plate to fit standard lamp types, such as E27 screw or BC22 bayonet
- two fixing screws suitable for wood – to match the size of your lamp holder and 1cm in length
- bulb to match lamp holder
- 2m of 3-core cable (normal electrical cable with an earth wire – ask at the DIY store that it is suitable for the lamp holder you have selected)
- wood glue
- standard plug
- seven pieces of 6mm x 6mm square-section wood the same length as the longest side of your box
- sixteen 13mm panel pins
- sheet of plywood for lamp guard measuring half the box length by box width

From art shop
- three sheets of heavy-weight watercolour paper big enough to cover the open front of the box with 1cm extra border
- sheet of graph paper (same size as watercolour paper)
- masking tape or sticky tape

What to do

1. Prepare the box by taking out any unnecessary fixings with pliers. Then remove stickers, clean with a damp cloth and sand down.
2. On the shorter side of the box, measure the mid-point and from here draw a pencil line to the back of the box. Find the point one quarter of the way along this line from the back of the box (fig A), and drill a hole here with the 8mm drill bit. This is for the cable to go through, so check that it fits before proceeding!

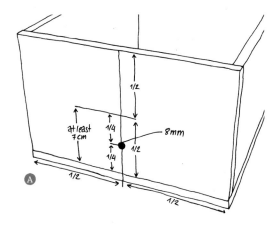

3. Centre the lamp holder base over the hole on the inside of the box. With a pencil, mark where the screw positions will be (fig B). With the 2mm or 3mm drill bit, drill holes for the screws going around three quarters of the way through the wood.

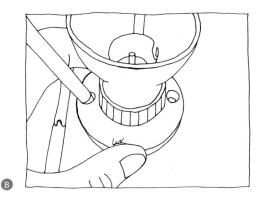

4. With the pozidriv screwdriver and the fixing screws, screw the lamp holder inside the box.
5. Measure seven lengths of square-section wood to fit inside the long side of the box. Cut the lengths with a saw (or craft knife if you don't have one); then sand the ends smooth. Cut one section in half.
6. Run a spare piece of square-section wood along one of the inside corners of the box. Find the mid-point (in depth), and in the top half of the depth mark out three 6mm-wide sections about 1cm apart, with one close to the edge of the box. Use this as a template to mark out, at either end of the two longer sides of the box, where the six long square-section runners will go (fig C).

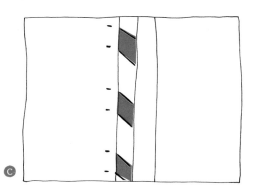

7. Line up the long lengths of square-section with the pencil marks, so htat they run parallel to the edge of the box and lightly hammer in a panel pin at each end – do this carefully to make sure the wood doesn't split. Place the two half-lengths about 6mm underneath the last runner, on the side of the lamp holder, and hammer into place (fig D).

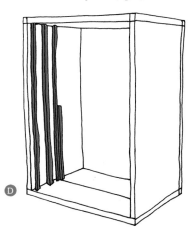

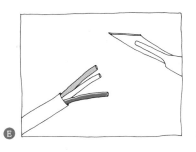

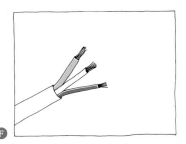

8. Now for the wiring. Use a craft knife to carefully score around the cable 3cm from the end and remove the outer cover, making sure the internal wires are intact (fig E).
9. Then strip the cover carefully off the separate wires 6mm from the ends (fig F). Twist the exposed copper wires together on each strip. (If you are not confident doing this, ask someone to help, or look it up online.)

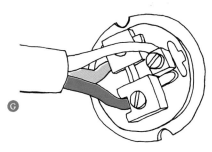

10. Now to wire up the electrical connections in the lamp holder. The live wire is brown, blue is neutral, and the green and yellow wire is the earth. The live and neutral wires go into the matching contacts, while earth goes in the separate connector (fig G). If in any doubt, please check with someone that you have it wired correctly. Using a flat-headed screwdriver, unscrew the electrical contacts enough to push the wires into place, then screw tight again and pull to check they are secure.
11. Once you are happy that the wiring is safe and secure, thread the other end of the cable through the hole to the outside of the box and screw in the lamp holder (fig H).

12. Next to wire the plug at the other end of the cable: open up the plug with a screwdriver and strip the cable as before. Strip the individual cables to 6mm of bare copper wire, and twist. Wire the plug as shown on the diagram it is supplied with (fig I). Make sure you have wired it correctly and all connections are secure before closing the plug.

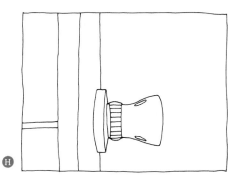

13. Insert the bulb into the lamp holder; plug it in and switch it on. Hopefully it will emit light!
14. To make the lamp guard, measure the short inner width of the box and the total height of the lamp. Add 3cm to the lamp height, and cut out a piece of wood to these measurements. Along one edge that is the same length as the shorter inner width of the box, you can cut out a cloud-like edge, or any other effect you like. Sand down the edges.

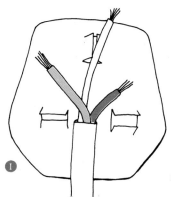

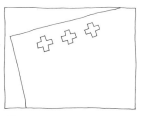

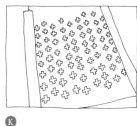

J   K

15. Glue along the front-facing edge of the short square-section runners and slot the lamp guard in front. Hold against the glue and allow to dry. This will make sure the lamp and paper don't come into contact.

16. To make the paper screen, measure the box's inner dimensions of width and length, add a border of 2cm to the width of the box and cut out three sheets of watercolour paper to this size with ruler and craft knife.

17. Then cut a piece of graph paper the same size (or stick some pieces together to make this size): this will be used as a template for the pattern-cutting.

18. Decide on a shape you would like to use to make a pattern – this version uses small crosses. They should be fairly small, about 2cm x 2cm, to avoid making the paper too floppy. On the graph paper, mark out the 1cm border along both width lengths; then draw out the shapes (fig J). Leave at least 1cm of paper at the edge of the design (plus the 1cm borders) and repeat the shape (altering the spacing for a slightly more random pattern) until it fills the whole paper.

19. Place the cutting mat on a firm surface; then layer one piece of watercolour paper with the graph paper lined up neatly on top. Tape the graph paper in place (fig K).

20. Using a sharp blade, cut through the graph and watercolour papers along the lines of the pattern.

21. Remove the graph paper and push out the shapes; you might need to cut into some of the corners again to do this. Fold over the 1cm borders along the long edges and slot these folded sections in between the two long runners closest to the lamp.

22. Turn on the lamp to see the effect the first layer has created. There is another space at the front where you can add further paper layers. This version has cut cloud shapes into two more pieces of paper, and overlapped them at the front (fig L). You could also cut out more patterns too, just remember to keep the 1cm borders along the width edges intact for folding into the slot. For safety reasons, don't add too many layers of paper; you need to make sure there is enough space for air to circulate for cooling. Also, ensure that the paper doesn't touch the lamp at any point.

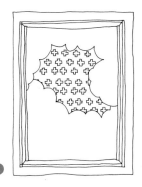

L

TIP
The light box is not protected against dust, so after a while you might have to give it a clean, or you can make some new paper cuts... think of it as your own miniature theatre set.

Hannah Wardle is a freelance lighting designer living in east London who can't get away from the fact that she likes making stuff, and so has been making some laser-cut things. *www.hannahwardle.com. www.etsy.com/shop/hannahchristie.*

Maris Schiess' **Water-Pistol Lights**

A super-simple, plastic-fantastic project to shoot up some light.

What to do

1. Pull out the tabs on the side of the water-pistols that are used to fill the gun up with water. Place the bulbs into these holes.
2. Stretch out a paperclip, or cut a short piece of plastic-coated wire, and simply twist the paper clip around the water-pistol tab and the light wire (fig A). Make sure the twist is tight enough that the gun will not fall out. Hang up: it's that simple!

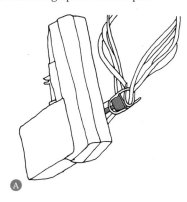

Ⓐ

Materials
~ strand of fairy lights
~ cheap toy water-pistols – one for each bulb
~ paperclips – again, one for each bulb – in the same color as the wire of the lights. You can use other plastic-coated wire, such as green garden wire, which is the same colour as the wire of Christmas-tree lights

Maris Schiess is an advertising student waiting to break out into the creative world. Creating unique crafts to enhance her room and her style serves as a stress reliever, boredom avoider and an enjoyable hobby. No matter where her studies may lead her, arts and crafts will always be a big part of her life. *www.twitter.com/meschiess*.

Custom Made's **Giant Cushions**

By Anna Butler

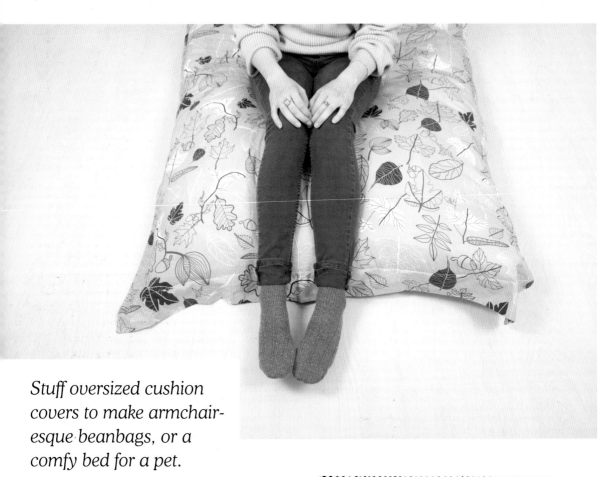

Stuff oversized cushion covers to make armchair-esque beanbags, or a comfy bed for a pet.

Tools

- ~ dressmakers' pins
- ~ tailors' chalk, or a pencil
- ~ scissors
- ~ iron
- ~ sewing machine

Materials

- ~ 3.6m of fabric at least 1.6m wide (or 2.8m of 1.2m-wide fabric for the smaller version), such as a heavyweight cotton or canvas
- ~ approx 0.28 cubic metre of beanbag beans (or 0.23 cubic metre for the smaller version)
- ~ 46cm zip
- ~ sewing thread to match fabric

What to do

1. Cut two fabric panels to form the back and the front of the cushion. For the extra large version, you need two pieces measuring 160cm x 180cm; for the smaller version they should be 120cm x 140cm.
2. On both pieces, sew along one of the shorter edges with a zigzag stitch (if your fabric is patterned, this edge should be the one at bottom of the pattern).
3. Fold over these neatened edges, from right side to wrong side, by about 1.5cm, and press with an iron.

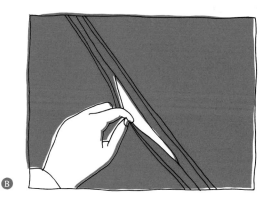

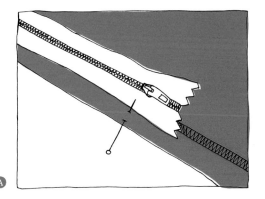

4. Measure along one neatened edge to find the middle of the fabric; place the centre of the zip at this point and mark with a pin through the fabric only (not the zip). This will ensure you get your zip right in the middle of the panel. Use two more pins to mark both ends of the zip (fig A); place the pins in the fabric just slightly further in (towards the centre of the zip) than the zip pull and the metal stopper – this will ensure the zip is well concealed at both ends and there are no openings for beans to escape.
5. Place the two pieces of fabric together, with the right sides facing. Unfold the seam allowance along the two neatened edges, and line up. Pin along this edge, making sure that the two end-zip pins stay in place. You can remove the pin that marks the middle.

6. Sew a straight line 1.5cm from the fabric edge (in the ironed crease) up to the pin that marks one end of the zip – make sure to back tack (sew backwards and then forwards again for 2cm or so) to make the seams strong at either end. Repeat from the other side to the other end-zip pin.
7. Press this seam open (with one layer of seam allowance over to either side), both where it is sewn and along the zip opening (fig B).
8. Open out the fabric with the wrong side facing upwards and the two edges of the zip opening close together. Matching the zip up with its marker pins, place it, teeth facing down, along the opening. Pin the zip in place (fig C).

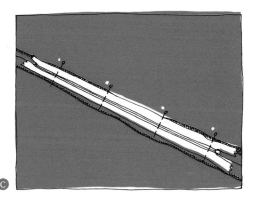

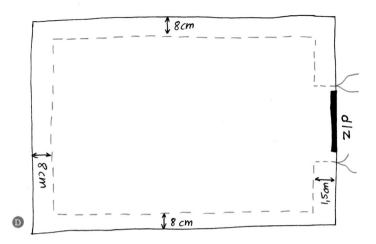

9. Turn the fabric over to the right side and make sure the seams, pins and opening are flat. On the right side, sew around the zip 0.5cm from the opening, using a zip foot if you have one. Be sure to reverse a couple of times over the ends of the zip to make this seam as strong as possible. Press lightly.

10. Open the zip. Folding over the zip seam, place the right sides of the fabric together and pin around the three remaining sides. Stitch along these three sides 1.5cm from the fabric edge of the panel.

11. Turn the bag right side out and press the seams flat. You are going to topstitch around the sides (but not over the top of the zip, of course) to make a nice border. With tailors chalk, draw the border as follows: starting at the edge, 1cm to the left-hand side of the zip, draw up 1.5cm; then turn to the left and draw straight along (keeping 1.5cm from the edge) to a point 8cm from the long edge in front. Repeat at the other end of the zip, to the right-hand side. Now draw a border along the three other sides, 8cm from the edge (fig D). Stitch all along this line, starting at the fabric edge to the left of the zip and turning at the corners with the needle in the fabric.

12. Now the bag is ready to fill. The beanbag beads are very static and seem to pour more easily through a cardboard tube.

> **TIP**
> Make regular-sized cushions in the same way – just add a 1.5cm seam allowance to the size of your cushion pad to work out the size of your two pieces of fabric, and leave out the border.

Anna Butler started sewing at a very early age, taught by her mum, who was taught by her mum – she comes from a long line of sewers! After a degree in fashion design, she worked as a menswear designer for six years. Itchy feet and a desire to do something else led her to set up Custom Made, selling handmade goodies and keeping hand-crafting alive. *www.custommadeuk.com*.

Craftivist Collective's
Mini Protest Banner

Make a statement in a creative, non-threatening way with some craftivism (activism through craft).

Tools

- ~ embroidery needle
- ~ tapestry needle
- ~ scissors
- ~ embroidery hoop (optional)
- ~ pinking shears (optional)
- ~ eyelet pliers, or a hammer
- ~ camera

Materials

- ~ 12cm x 17cm piece of 14-count cotton Aida cross-stitch fabric
- ~ embroidery thread in various colours
- ~ approx 20cm x 25cm piece of cotton fabric – the more colourful or kitsch the pattern, the more the banner will be noticed
- ~ embellishments if desired
- ~ two 4mm eyelets
- ~ two 3.6mm x 15cm cable ties
- ~ sheet of squared paper
- ~ Craftivist Collective label (optional)

Skills

- ~ cross-stitch

What to do

1. Think about the human rights issues that you feel strongly about and decide on a fact/slogan/quote for your mini protest banner. You can find up-to-date statistics on the UN website or contact Craftivist Collective to get some ideas. Plot out the slogan on squared paper, in an area no bigger than 10cm x 15cm. You can use straight lines along the edges of the squares to form words, or rows of "x"s filling the squares (see page 38).

2. Gather together all the materials you need in a small bag to make the banner in a public place – café, train, bus, park bench – so if people ask you what you are doing, you can talk about the injustice your mini protest banner is trying to raise awareness of.

3. Cut a length of thread about 30cm long. Separate the six strands of the thread in half, using only three strands at all times. Start in the centre of the Aida and the centre of your pattern, and cross-stitch your message.

4. Draw a rectangle around the message, leaving at least a 1cm space from the stitching, and cut out.

5. Place the cross-stitch on top of the cotton fabric, in the centre, and pin in place. If you have pinking shears, cut round the edge of the fabric leaving a 2cm-3cm border – or a wider space if you want to embellish with buttons, ribbons, sequins, beads etc – around the cross-stitch message (fig A). Alternatively, hem the edges so they don't fray: turn about 1cm of the fabric over at the back; fold the fabric over again to hide the rough edge, then sew in place with a running stitch.

6. Sew around the Aida onto the fabric using three strands of embroidery thread in a blanket stitch or whipstitch.

7. In the top two corners of the mini protest banner, you need to add a 4mm eyelet to thread cable ties through. If you have eyelet pliers, punch a hole out of each top corner with them and then punch in the eyelets. If you do not have eyelet pliers, make a small slit into each corner and push the eyelets through; with a hammer on a firm surface, hit the eyelets until they are flush over the fabric (fig B).

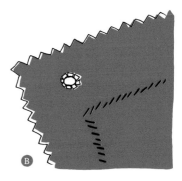

B

8. Sew a Craftivist Collective label (or homemade label) onto the banner, so that people will be able to find more information about your Craftivist protest online.

9. Add any embellishments you desire. For example, you could add fashion symbols such as scissors, buttons and tape-measure ribbon if your protest is about unethical fashion; or food symbols if you are campaigning against unfair trade rules.

10. Now decide the best location for the mini protest banner: somewhere with a high footfall that is also relevant to your cause. So, near high street stores if you are campaigning on fair trade, or near a park if you are passionate about saving the planet.

11. Bring the two cable ties and a pair of scissors to your location. Thread the cable ties through the eyelets and around a lamppost or some railings.

12. Take a photograph of your work, then write up a blog about your mini protest: why you picked a certain location and information on the cause you are passionate about. Email the photo and the blog to *craftivist-collective@hotmail.com*, and look out for it being posted on *www.craftivist-collective.com*.

A

There is a gap in the clouds of unbridled capitalism, now's the time to act for **justice**

Love from Craftivist Collective

London-based Sarah Corbett brought together her passion for craft and her passion for fighting global injustices in a blog called A Lonely Craftivist and in her Craftivism project. For her, craftivism is a personal reaction against more aggressive forms of activism, which she is not comfortable with. You can spot mini protest banners all over the world, made by a growing collective of craftivists spanning from London, Manchester and Glasgow to Copenhagen, Berlin, LA and Quebec. *www.craftivist-collective.com, www.YouTube.com/CraftivistCollective.*

D.S.Lookkin's **Geometric Earrings**

Perfect for crochet practice; beginner-sized bits can be transformed into modish accessories.

Tools
~ 3.75mm crochet hook
~ 2.75mm crochet hook, or yarn needle
~ scissors, or pinking shears

Materials
~ any aran-weight acrylic yarn
~ felt scraps
~ earring backs/studs
~ cardboard and paper scraps
~ strong all-purpose glue (or you can use a glue gun if you have one)

Crochet skills
Triangle
~ chain
~ slip stitch
~ decrease

Circle
~ chain
~ slip stitch
~ double crochet
~ working in the round
~ increase

What to do

1. Crochet either a triangle or a circle according to the following patterns. Make sure you leave a tail of yarn at least 10cm long when you make your starting slipknot.

Triangle

Row 1: using the 3.75mm hook, 10ch. Turn.
Row 2: sk1, sl st to last st. Turn.
Row 3: place the hook in the opening directly next to the hook under both loops. Sl st to last st. Turn. You'll start to see curly bumps on the sides – this is supposed to happen.
Rows 4–9: Repeat Row 3 until there are no rows left. It should end with a point (fig A). Fasten off. Cut the yarn with a 10cm tail and pull tight to form pointy triangle corners.

Circle

Row 1: using the 3.75mm hook, 5ch. Join in a circle by placing the hook behind the knot. As you work, the right side of your finished project will be facing you.
Row 2: 10dc to centre.
Row 3: 2dc into each st. (20 sts).

Row 4: 1dc into each st. (20 sts). To finish and round out the circle, make 2 slip stitches into just one loop of next two stitches (fig B). Fasten off.

2. Make two shapes and weave away the yarn ends on the wrong side of the piece. You can use the smaller crochet hook, pushing it into stitch loops one at a time and pulling the tail through, or work the ends through the back of the stitches with a yarn needle. Trim yarn ends.

3. Draw around one of the shapes on a scrap of paper and cut it out about 0.5cm smaller all around. Lay it on the circles/triangles: it should fit within the shapes with a small border.

4. Place the paper shape on the felt and cut around it with scissors or pinking shears. Make a second felt shape. These will make a backing to the earrings.

5. Place some cardboard scraps under the crochet shapes, which should be facing wrong side up. Spread a small amount of glue in the middle of both triangles/circles and place the felt in the desired position, pushing it down gently. If some glue oozes out of the sides, scoop it up with a scrap of cardboard. Leave to dry for at least an hour.

6. Now glue the earring posts to the felt: for the circle, it should be just off-centre below where you finished crocheting this piece; for the triangle, it should be near the top point. Place a bead of glue on the flat end of the post and push onto the felt; hold till secure, then leave to dry for an hour.

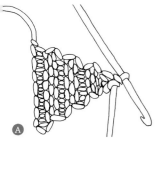

(A)

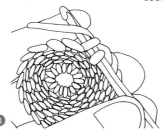

(B)

Dawn Stewart-Lookkin was born and raised in New York City and has always loved to make things, from mixed-media sculptures to paintings. With her brand, d.s.lookkin, Dawn creates wearable art with crochet. She lives with her boyfriend/domestic partner/best friend in Jackson Heights, Queens, and they both sing and perform with Rev Billy & The Church of Earthalujah, a radical street-theatre troupe. *www.dslookkin.com, www.etsy.com/shop/dslookkin, www.revbilly.com.*

Big Jumper Pouffe

By Victoria Woodcock

Wonderful woollen seating that swallows up unwanted fabric items.

Tools

~ dressmakers' pins
~ 50cm piece of string
~ ruler
~ tape measure
~ scissors
~ sewing machine

Final size

~ 60cm x 26cm

Materials

~ a very large jumper, with a front body area at least 56cm x 74cm and an arm 42cm around. If you can't find one this big, use two. Make the pattern pieces (steps 1-6) before you go jumper hunting
~ 120cm x 120cm of cotton fabric for lining; an old bed sheet would be ideal
~ sewing thread
~ lots of stuffing such old pillows, towels, clothes, bedding etc, or you can buy foam pieces or polyester fibre fill
~ two A2-size pieces of thin paper, such as newsprint

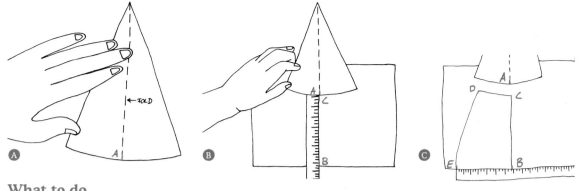

What to do

1. First you need to plot out your pattern. On the newsprint, draw out a circle approx 38cm in diameter. The way to do this is to measure and mark out 19cm along a piece of string. At these points, tie the string to two pencils; don't tie the knots too tightly, so that the pencils can rotate in the loops. Place one pencil in the centre of the paper, holding it perpendicular, and hold the other one out so that the string is taut and sits at the same height on each pencil; rotate the second pencil around the central one, keeping it upright.

2. Fold the circle in half, quarters and then eighths, being as accurate as you can. Fold one section in half again to find the midpoint of this curve, and unfold (fig A). This halfway point along the curve is point A.

3. Fold another piece of paper in half. Mark a point at roughly the midpoint of this fold (point B), and draw a line at a right angle to the fold, measuring 15cm. This is point C.

4. Place the folded circle at the top of this line, lining up point A and point B, and creating a continuous straight line between the drawn line on the paper and the fold on the circle (fig B).

5. Mark one corner of the circle section, point D, and trace the curve of the folded circle between C and D. Then, on the same side as point D, mark out a point along the folded edge 12cm away from point B (this is point E). Join point D and point E with a gentle curved line to form a shape as shown in fig C.

6. Now fold along the line from B to C and cut out the shape (from C to D to E) through all four layers of paper. This and the circle are your two pattern pieces (fig D).

7. Now to dissect the jumper. Remove one arm and cut along the seam at the bottom to form one flat piece. Repeat with the other arm. Cut down one side of the body and along the shoulder either side of the neck. This will now fold out to one large section.

8. Place the circle on one of the arm pieces. Pin and cut out 1cm away from the pattern edge. Repeat on the other arm.

9. You want to make eight side panels, cutting out four from the front and four from the back of the jumper. Work out where you need to place the pattern piece to fit all four in. Pin and cut out 1cm from the pattern edge eight times.

10. Now cut out two circles and eight side panels in the same way from the cotton fabric, lining up the paper pieces with the grain and cutting 1cm around the pattern.

11. Place the lining pieces on the wrong side of the jumper pieces and pin in place. Tack the two layers together with a basting stitch about 0.5cm from the edge, either by hand or machine. Do this on every piece.

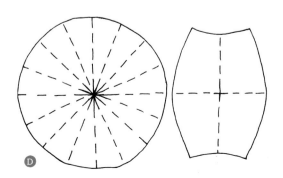

12. Now you want to sew the side panels together. Place one piece on top of another with the right sides of the jumper together in the centre and the linings facing outwards; pin along one of the long edges (with the pins at right angles to the edge). Sew a straight machine stitch 1cm from the edge (fig E), carefully following the curve, and remembering to back tack at either end of the seam.

13. Add another side panel to the two you've just sewn together. Line up two long edges in the same way, with the right sides of the jumper facing inwards. Sew along the curve.

14. Repeat step 13 until all eight panels are joined. They will curve round into a doughnut shape (fig F).

15. Now for the tricky-ish bit. You need to work the panel section around the circle. Place one circle in front of you, jumper side facing up. Now lie the panel on top, jumper side facing down, lining up the middle of the far edge with the edge of the circle furthest away from you. Pin at this point (fig G).

16. Now work the scalloped edge around the circle from this point, curling the panel edge to fit the curve of the circle and always lining up the edges carefully. Repeat around the other side of the circle. The ends of the panel section will meet at the opposite edge of the circle with 1cm allowance on either side.

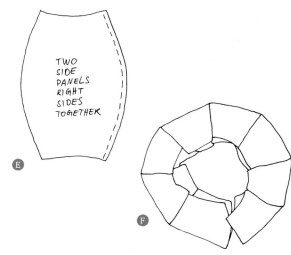

TWO SIDE PANELS RIGHT SIDES TOGETHER

E

F

17. Make sure the pieces are pinned securely all the way around then tack around the circle with a basting stitch. With the panel side facing up so that you can move the excess fabric out of the way of the needle, sew around the circle, starting at the gap, 1cm in from the edge of the first panel piece. The more uniform this circular seam, the neater your pouffe will look. So if you wobble, re-sew and unpick the uneven seam.

18. Repeat steps 15-17 at the other scalloped edge with the second circle (fig H). Then turn right side out.

19. Stuff your pouffe nice and full! With a small, neat whipstitch, start sewing the two panel sections together either side of the gap, folding the rough edges inwards by about 1cm as you go (fig I). Keep adding bits of stuffing to round out the seam.

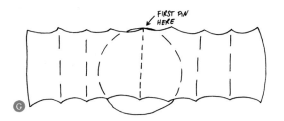

FIRST PIN HERE

G

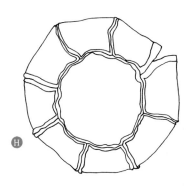

H

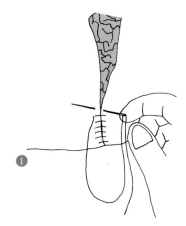

I

Teacakes and 78s'
Over-The-Top Tea Cosies

By Angel Ashcroft

Make a statement at teatime with woolly wonders to warm your brew.

The tea cosy

Tools

~ dressmakers' pins
~ yarn needle
~ pair of 5mm knitting needles
~ tape measure
~ set of compasses
~ good sharp scissors

What to do

1. Using 5mm knitting needles, cast on 40 sts. The cosy is knitted in a knit-1-purl-1 rib throughout.
2. Work the pattern as follows:
   Row 1: k1, p1 to end (make sure you always end on a purl stitch).
   Row 2: k1, p1 to end (also ending on a purl stitch).
   Repeat these two rows until piece measures 15cm (if your teapot is a bit taller than 15cm, keep on knitting to that height).
3. Now work 5 rows with decreases to shape the top of the cosy as follows:
   Row 1: *k2tog; rep from * to end. You now have 20 sts remaining.
   Row 2: knit every stitch.
   Row 3: *k2tog; rep from * to end. You now have 10 sts.
   Row 4: knit every stitch.
   Next Row: *k2tog; repeat from to end.
   Cast off the remaining 5 sts.
4. Repeat steps 1-3 to make the other side of cosy.
5. Place the two halves together, lining up the cast-on edges. You are going to sew up the side seams, but first mark out with pins where the gaps need to be to accommodate the spout and handle of your teapot (fig A). Then, with a yarn needle and a strand the same wool, sew up the seams with a mattress stitch.

Materials

~ 100g ball of double-knit wool yarn such as Knitting4Fun's Felting Wool in Periwinkle

Knit skills

~ cast on
~ knit, purl and rib
~ decrease
~ cast off
~ mattress stitch

Gauge

~ An exact gauge is not essential; the cosy is ribbed to stretch and fit most standard size (about 15cm-high) teapots

Pom-Pom Extravaganza

....

Materials
~ cardboard, such as a cereal box
~ any yarns you like – the pompom pictured was made using Rowan Cocoon in Seascape (blue) and Shale (grey) with a burst of Malabrigo Fucsia (pink)

What to do

1. Draw out two circles roughly 13cm in diameter, and draw a smaller 4cm-diameter hole in the middle of each. Cut out to form doughnut-shaped discs.
2. Create your super-large pom-pom with these discs following the instructions on page 28.
3. Sew the pom-pom onto the top of the tea cosy – use plenty of stitches as it will be pretty heavy.

Mr Octopus

....

Tools
~ sewing needle
~ 5mm crochet hook

....

Crochet skills
~ chain
~ slip stitch
~ double crochet
~ working in rounds
~ increasing/decreasing

....

Materials
~ 100g ball of double-knit wool yarn (such as Knitting4Fun's Felting Wool in Aqua Grey)
~ small amount of stuffing or ends of wool to stuff the octopus
~ two black beads for eyes
~ black sewing thread

What to do

1. First for the legs: crocheted tubes that can then be stuffed with oddments of wool. Make eight of them using the 5mm crochet hook as follows:
   Rnd 1: 3ch, sl st into first chain to form a loop. 1ch counts as first dc, 3dc into loop.
   Rnd 2: *1 dc into next dc, 2 dc in next dc; repeat from * once. (You now have 6 sts.)
   Now continue working 1 dc into each dc until piece measures 17cm. Fasten off.
2. And now for the body:
   Again, using the 5mm hook, 3ch, sl st into first chain to form a loop.
   Rnd 1: 6dc into loop, join with a sl st into first dc.
   Rnd 2: 2dc into each of the 6 dc (12 sts).
   Rnd 3: *1dc, 2dc into next dc; rep from * 6 times (18 sts).
   Rnd 4: *1dc into next 2dc, 2dc into next dc; rep from * 6 times (24 sts).
   Rnd 5: *1dc into each of the next 3dc, 2dc into next dc; rep from * 6 times (30 sts).
   Rnd 6: *1dc into next 4dc, 2dc into next dc; rep from * 6 times (36 sts).
   Rnds 7-12: 1dc into every dc.
   Rnd 13: *1dc into next 4dc, skip 1dc; rep from * 6 times (30 sts).
   Rnd 14: *1dc into next 3 sts, skip 1dc; rep from *6 times (24 sts).
   Rnd 15: *1dc into next 2 sts, skip 1dc; rep from * 6 times (18 sts).
   Rnd 16: *1dc, sk1, 1dc; rep from * 6 times (12 sts).
   Rnd 17: *1dc, sk1, 1dc; rep from * 6 times (6 sts).
   Fasten off.
3. Stuff the body with scraps of wool or stuffing, and sew closed. Stuff the legs and sew them onto the body, about 4cm up from the bottom.
4. Using a length of that yarn that you used for the tea cosy body (or another scrap you have lying around), sew on a mouth. Sew the beads on as eyes.
5. With a length of wool and the yarn needle, attach the octopus body to the top of the cosy. Place the cosy on your teapot and arrange the legs, curling them in interesting positions. Sew these into place with few stitches at the bottom of the legs.

"Mr Octopus is one of Teacakes and 78s best-loved tea cosy designs – he always receives much love at craft fairs."

Teacakes and 78s is the rock n' roll brainchild of Angel Ashcroft and Toby Thurston, who are inspired by vintage fabrics and hand-spun wools. In a desperate attempt to hide their obsessions with buying these items, they decided to make things using them and sell them on. They dream up ideas and colour combinations into one-off items that make people happy. Cake, riot grrrl and a DIY ethics are all inspirations for their creations. *www.teacakesand78s.co.uk.*

Templates

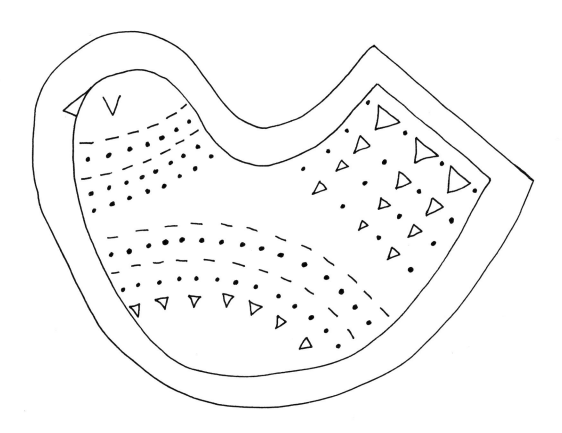

Mr Wingate's **Dazzling 3-D Tee** ~ page 92

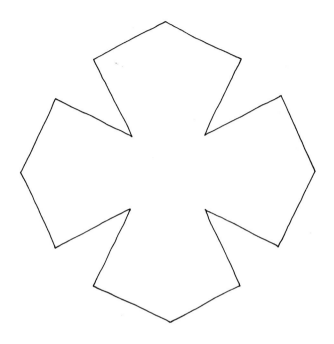

Erin Dollar's **Mysterious Moustache Disguise** ~ page 106

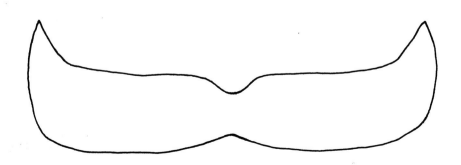

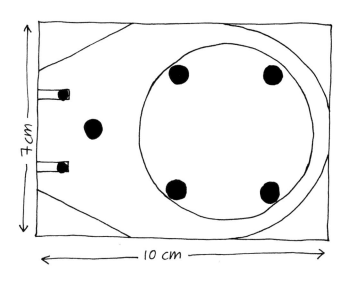

7 cm

10 cm

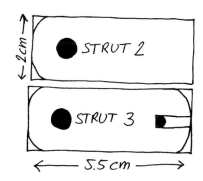

2 cm

STRUT 2

STRUT 3

5.5 cm

STRUT 1

25 cm

* These templates are scaled to 80 per cent of the actual size.

Lizzybeth's Felties' **Mr Sailor Whale Purse** ~ page 122

I Heart…'s **See You Soon Card** ~ page 157

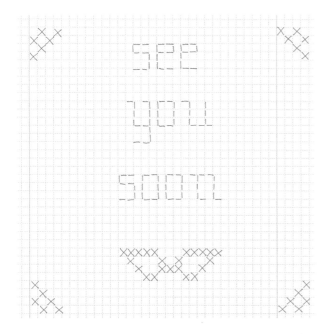

* These templates are scaled to 80 per cent of the actual size.

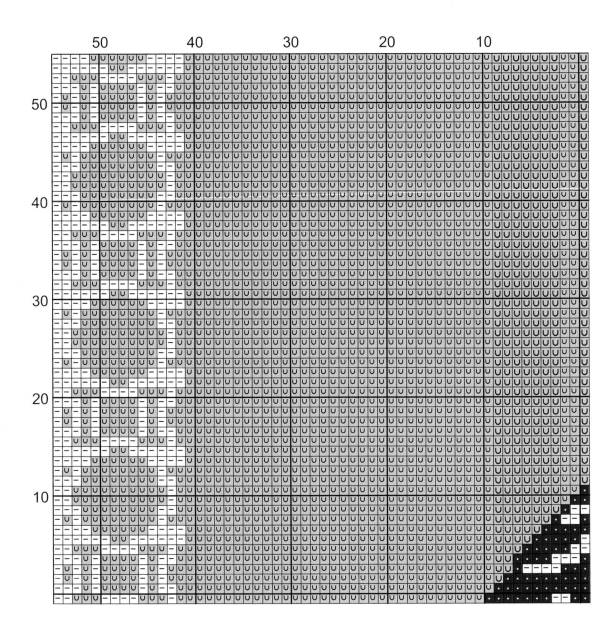

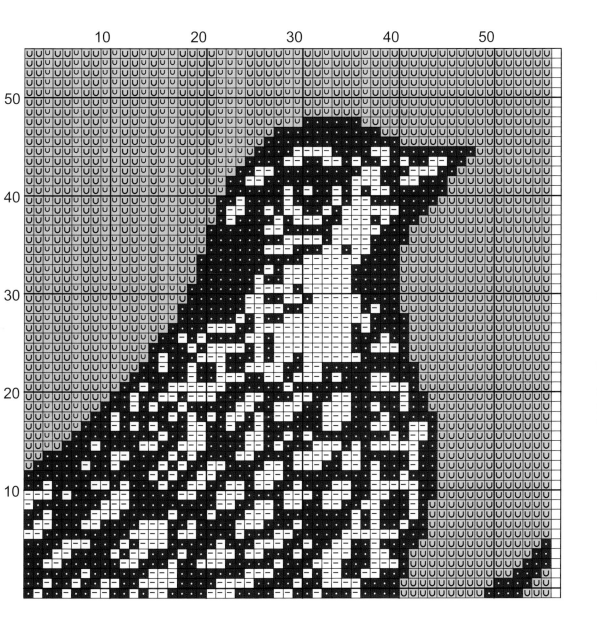

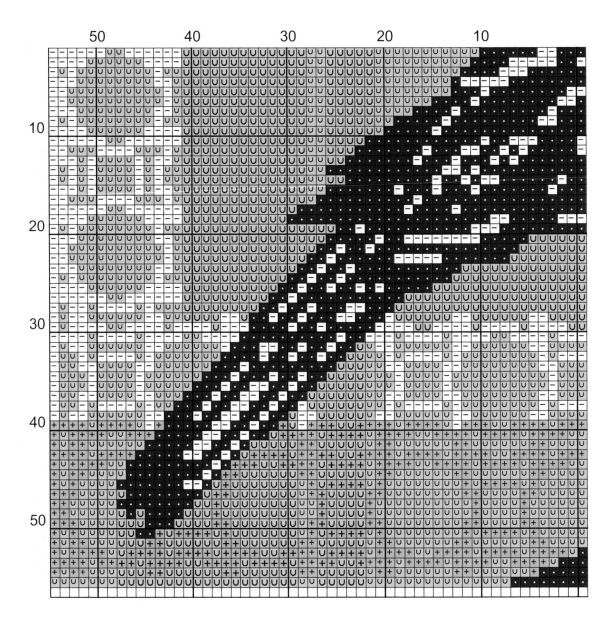

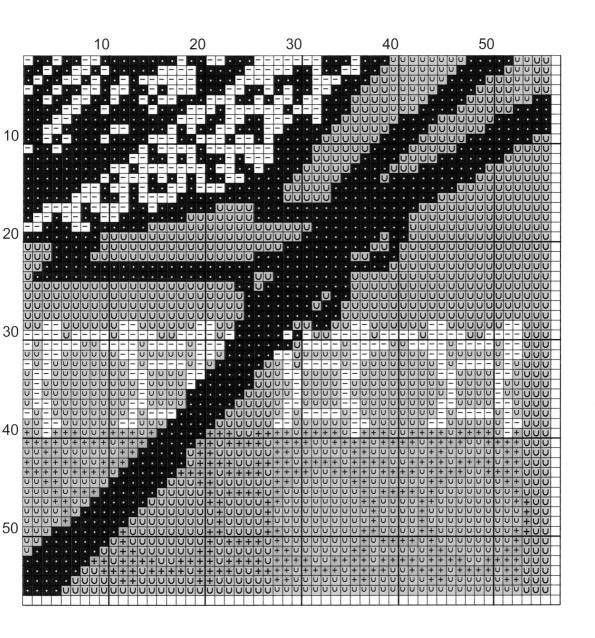

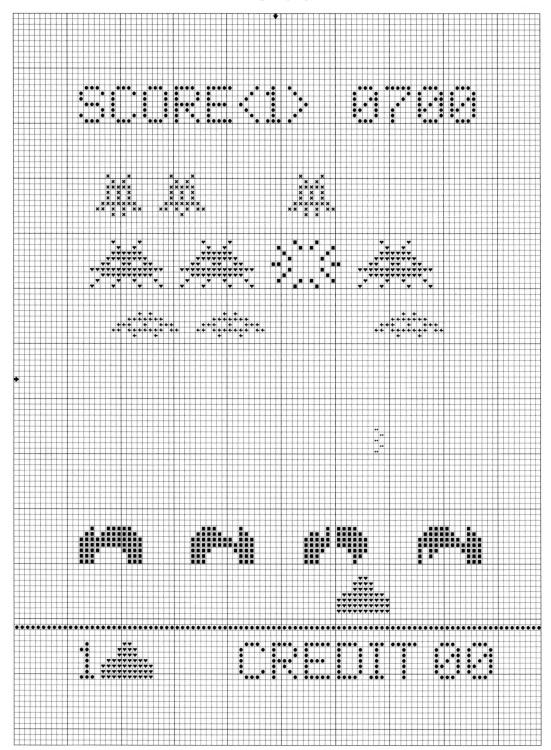

Floss used for full stitches

◻	●	2	Anchor	1	Snow White
◼	♥	2	Anchor	185	Sea Green LT
◻	◆◆	2	Anchor	290	Canary Yellow Med
◼	←	2	Anchor	410	Electric Blue DK
◼	✕	2	Anchor	871	Amethyst Med LT
◼	◼	2	Anchor	1098	Crimson Red LT

Naomi Ryder's **Couched Hummingbird** *~ page 191*

Acknowledgements

A big thank you to everyone that submitted an amazing project to State of Craft, who have all been a pleasure to work with and without whom, obviously, this book would not have been possible.

Many thanks to April for their fantastic flair – as well as their patience and diligence in designing this book, and to Katrin Zellmer who did such a brilliant job on all the illustrations.

Thanks also to Alex Bratt, Chloé Burrow, Coralie Sleap, Dave Hillier, Katie Bonham, Kristie Bishop, Louise Harries, Marianne Moore, Rachael Matthews, Elen Roberts and Sheila Burgel for lending their fine figures as top craft models; as well as to Drink, Shop & Do (www.drinkshopdo.com) and Prick Your Finger (www.prickyourfinger.com) for providing locations and Catherine Waterfield for her help with the crochet projects.

Victoria Woodcock would also like to thank Garry Maclennan for traipsing down to London on the Mega Bus and being so easy to work with; Vicki Reeve for being the most understanding of bosses; Ziggy Hanaor at Cicada Books for above all being a good friend; and Dave Hillier for all the love and support (and the spaghetti Bolognaise).

Wig blocks by kind permission of Ede & Ravenscroft, Chancery Lane.

Rowan Big Wool for the Soft n' Mossy snood kindly supplied by Rowan yarns.

Published by Cicada Books Limited

Edited by Victoria Woodcock
Designed by April, www.studio-april.com
Photography by Garry Maclennan
Text and images by the contributors
as specified

British Library Cataloguing-in-Publication Data.

ISBN: 978-0-9562053-4-6

Cicada Books Limited
76 Lissenden Mansions
Lissenden Gardens
London, NW5 1PR

T: +44 207 267 5208
E: ziggy@cicadabooks.co.uk
W: www.cicadabooks.co.uk